The Divine Garland

Commentary on Goda Devi's 30 Pasurams

INDICA

The Divine Garland

Commentary on Goda Devi's 30 Pasurams

KUNTIMADDI SESHASARMA
English translation by Dr. K. Sadananda

INDICA

SHREE KUNTIMADDI SESHASARMA

CONTENTS

PREFACE

This work is based on my father's extensive commentary in Telugu on the *Tiruppavai*. The book was entitled '*Meli Nomu*' and was published by Tirupati Tirumala Devasthanam (TTD). The first publication came out in 1991, and the second one in 2003. It is currently out of print. In this book, I am providing my free English translation of his commentary on the Tiruppavai. The English translation does not project the original literary beauty of his commentary but hopefully could provide a glimpse of my father's philosophical and devotional offerings. With prostrations at his holy feet, I am daring to venture into this. Of course, a big push also came from my wife, a Vishishtadvaitin at heart, for doing this.

Our families are originally from Tirumala, with *Shatamaharshan Gotram*. In the Vaishnava community, we are normally referred to as Tirumala people. Our forefathers moved out of Tirumala and settled in various villages in Rayalaseema when they were given some land. In the process, they picked up the village name as the family name. Thus, we became Kuntimaddi family. Krishnadevaraya's guru, Tirumala Tatacharyulu apparently is one of our ancestors.

The Tirumala people are known for their scholarships. There are many Ashtavadanis and Shatavadanis in our family. Our ninth great, great-grandfather had written a shatakam (a hundred slokas) in Sanskrit on Lakshmi Devi. My father found that work written on leaves in the attic of one of our relatives, but in a poor condition. He rewrote it, filling up the missing words or lines damaged by the insects, with his commentary on it. He considered that the work was scholarly since each sloka depicts several *alankaras* or similes.

My father has written many books both in Sanskrit and Telugu. TTD has published many of his works. The works include the Sanskrit translation of Amukata Malyada of Shree Krishnadevaraya which depicts the story of Goda Devi, also known as Shree Andal, the author of this Tiruppavai. He introduced Telugu chandas into Sanskrit, such as Seesam, Ataveladi, Tetageeta, Kandam, etc., with their characteristic yati and praasa. Many of his books are on Vishishtadvaita. As the story goes, he was offered to head the Parakala Matt but declined it since he had to take up Sanyaasa. Several of his books remain unpublished. The notable one is his extensive commentary on Vedanta Desika's Tamil work, 'Rahasyatraya Saara'. My father studied Telugu and Sanskrit in Tirupati. But late in his life, he mastered Tamil and wrote the commentary on this Tiruppavai and also on Rahasyatraya saara.

We are seven children, but none of us could attain that scholarship. In fact, I have become an Advaitin under the guidance of my teacher Swami Chinmayanandaji.

Nevertheless, he was happy that I was devoting my time to the spiritual path. When he stayed with us in the States for a few months, he wrote his poetic commentary in Telugu on Bhagavat Geeta, following Shree Ramanuja's Shree Bhashya.

In this work, I got a lot of help from my siblings, Sudhasindhu and Sowdamini, ensuring that my quoted slokas and Telugu poems were correct. I am grateful to Shree Kaushik Chevendra, whom I met online on AdaitaL–list dedicated to discussions on Advaita, for writing the Introduction.

Thanks to Shree Hari Kiran Vadlamani, who volunteered to publish this book under the Indic Academy. Shree Hari Kiranji has done tremendous work in uplifting the Sananta Dharma, establishing Indic Academy, publishing many books, and providing Vedanta talks on YouTube by many notable scholars. He was also kind enough to publish my books; three volumes of 'Journey Beyond: A non-dual Approach,' 'Transcending Science,' and 'Self and The Supreme.' In addition, he made several of my talks on Vedanta available on YouTube under the name Acharya Sadaji. Let God's blessings shower on him for his noble efforts.

Finally, I want to thank my life partner, Mrinalini, who provides me with constant inspiration to make our lives, and those of others around, better. She is the embodiment of love and goes out of her way to help others who need it. She got all the Telugu Pasurams professionally recorded in the same style as MS Subbalakshmi. My brother-in-law, Shree Vinjamuri Subash, set them to music and played the violin. Smt. Kanaka Durga of Kuchipudi fame provided the singing. My wife also choreographed Kuchipudi Dance with my granddaughter, Laasya Sidhaye, dancing one pasuram a day during the last Margasira month.

This is to acknowledge that the Tamil script for the pasurams was taken from the website http://www.tiruppavai.net/index.html and the English transliteration from https://aanmeegam.co.in/blogs/thiruppavai-lyrics-english.

We feel it is the Goddess Andal's blessings that we could complete this translation of her Pasurams on the Lord.

– Hari Om!

Sadananda

Chennai, October 14, 2022.

A BRIEF HISTORY

Our Father, Shreeman Kuntimaddi Seshacharlu (pen-name Kuntimaddi Seshasarma), was born on August 22, 1913 to Shree Rangacharlu and Seshamma. Shree Rangacharlu was working as a lecturer at Rajamandri college and passed away when our father was just four years old. That was the time the nation was hit with a flu epidemic. My father was adopted by his uncle, yet grew up under the care of his Grandfather, Shree Shreenivasacharlu, in Ballari. My father introduces himself by acknowledging his grandfather in all his works as 'శేషశర్మ పేరు, శ్రీనివాసాచార్య పండితాగ్రగణ్య పౌత్రుడేను', praising his grandfather as great pandit. He and his elder brother, Raghavacharlu studied together in Tirupati and completed their Vidvan in Telugu, and Shiromani in Sanskrit. Shree Tirumala Ramachandra (ex. Editor of Andhra Prabha) and Puttaparthi Narayanacharlu (popularly known as Saraswati Putra in Telugu literature) were his classmates. With encouragement from Tirumala Ramachandra, my father started composing in Sanskrit and Telugu. While still a student, his first work was a translation into Sanskrit, the famous Telugu poetry, Sumati Shatakam. This work remains to be published. He got employed as Telugu Pandit in Penukonda when Shree Puttaparthi Sreenivasacharlu (father of Puttaparthi Narayanacharlu) retired from that post.

The famous Rallapalli Ananta Krishna Sarma, a well-known scholar in Telugu, Sanskrit, and Music, was his mentor. Shree Rallapalli has set to music many of the Annamacharya Keethanas. He also wrote 'Forward' to my father's first publication, 'Sudhabiduvulu.' Following that publication, our father has written many books and articles. The famous ones are the translation into Sanskrit Shree Krishnadevaraya's work, Amukta Malyada, which depicts the story of Goda Devi. Andhra Sahitya Academy published his book. He also translated the famous Allasani Peddana's Manucharitra into Sanskrit, which TTD published. Other works include a Telugu novel, 'Election చేసిన మేలు', 'అలంకార విచారము', scholarly discussions on the similes in Telugu and Sanskrit literature in the Bharati monthly magazine. Other works include Telugu Talli, Rami Reddy, Sindhuja Vandanam, etc. He wrote 'Parakala Matha Vaibhavam' at the request of local Vaishnavates and was facilitated by Parakala Mutt. The Mutt recognized him as their Poet. He has written many books on Vishishtadvaita, a series of books on the Spiritual Journey of Shree Ramanuja called Shree Yatirajeeyamu, etc. A complete list of books by our father was provided in my book 'Self and the Supreme' published by the Indic Academy. On Bhagavat Geeta, he wrote commentaries in prose, Geeta Amrutamu, and one in poetry, Geeta Navaneetam' following Shree Ramanuja's Shree Bhashya. To propagate the Shree Vaishnava doctrine, he translated the Tamil works 'Tiruppalandu' and 'Tiruppavai', the central theme of the current work. He has 14 volumes of commentary on Vedanta Deshika's 'Rahasyatraya Saaram', which remains unpublished. From Penukonda, he moved to Dharmavaram in 1960, where he continued his spiritual and literary contributions at the request of the local devotees. With the grace of the Lord, he composed a suprabhatam to Chennakeshava Swami (Maha Vishnu), Kehsava Prappatti, and also many poetic contributions such as Indira Vandanam, Vishishtadvaita Siddhanta Darpanamu, Shreemat Ramayana Paryavalochanamu, Sreenivas Kusumanjali, etc.

In our house, there were always some poetic discussions with visiting poets and scholars. Our mother, Smt. Jayalaksmi, made sure that the environment was maintained while taking care of their seven children, plus children of relatives who were staying there for studies, students from village Kuntimaddi who came and stayed in the house to complete their studies, and some poor young students who were coming on specific days of the week, on rotation. The house was run like an ashram, with everyone doing their assigned duties before they sit for their daily studies. Our father provided whatever finances we needed for our higher education. My parents surrendered completely at the feet of the Lord and served Him in whatever way they could. Our mother in 1995, and father in 1996 left us to serve the Lord in Vaikunta.

We have helped establish a poor Brahmin students hostel in our father's name, and it has been running for the past 25 years, taking care of poor students from out of town to come and stay to complete their education. The current book is an English translation of his commentary in Telugu on Tiruupavai, published by TTD. His several books remain unpublished, and with the blessings of the Lord, we pray that they will get published soon.

With Prostrations at the holly feet of our mother and father.

Children of Shree Kuntimaddi Seshacharlu and Smt. Jayalakshmi.

SHRADDHANJALI

I composed the following poems in Telugu, using Telugu chandas or meters in honor of my father in 1996, when He left this abode to join the Lord in Vaikunta. My mother's name was Smt. Jayalakshmi. She was the incarnation of Goddess, and she poured out her love on everyone that came in contact with her. She left this abode in 1995, just a year before my father did. I had composed some Sanskrit Slokas on her when she left us, and these were included in my book 'Self and the Supreme,' published by the Indic Academy. We are fortunate to have such a divine couple as our parents, and these poems express our reverence for them to a small way.

***

శ్రద్ధాంజలి

సీ|| పయనించె నీనాడు పరమాత్మ ధామకు
            తన జన్మ పరమ పావనము చేసి,
       రచియించె నెన్నియో రసికులందరు మెచ్చ
            ఆంధ్రగీర్వాణ భాషలలయందు,
       సంస్కృతించె తెలుగు సాహిత్యములనెన్నొ
            ఆంధ్రేతరులు కూడ ననుభవింప,
       ప్రకటించె శ్రీ విశిష్టాద్వైత సారము
            కావ్యప్రబంధ సుగంధి తోడ,

ఆ|| కుంటిమద్ది వంశ కుల రాజ తిలకుండు
శేషశర్మ పేర శోభతెచ్చె.
పుత్రపౌత్రులకును పరమార్థము తెలిపి,
విష్ణుపురము జేరె వైష్ణవుండు.

ఆ|| అన్న రాఘవ తన అండ సదా యుండ
కలసి మెలసి చదివిరెన్నొ కొదవ లేక
రామచంద్ర తిరుమల ప్రేరణ వలన
మొదటి కావ్య రచన మొదలు పెట్ట దలచె.

సీ|| ఉట్టూత లూగించె కోవిదోత్తములను
        సకల అలంకార చర్చ తోడ
సంతోషమొప్పించె సరస హృదయమందు
        సుస్సుధాబిందు శతమ్ము తోడ
కర్తవ్యమెరిగించె కార్యాధికులకును
        తెనుగు తల్లి విషమ స్థితిని తెలిపి
విశ్మయింపన్ జేసె వికసిత హృదయముల్
        రామిరెడ్డి మొదలు రచన తోడ.

ఆ|| అల్లసాని వారి మనుచరిత్రను కూడ
సంస్కృతంబు నందు సత్కరించె
కృష్ణదేవరాయ నాముక్తికంటును
విష్ణుచిత్తమందు వెల్లడించె.

తే|| నీలకంఠుని శాంతి విన్యాసములను
చాటిచెప్పె తేట తెనుగు నందు కూడ
శ్రీ యతీశ రామానుజ సచ్చరిత్ర
నంత శ్రీయతిరాజీయమందు నుడివె.

తే|| వైష్ణవ మతసారమునెల్ల వడియగట్టి
ఇందిరావందనమును, కేశవ ప్రపత్తి,
శ్రీవిశిష్టమద్వైత దర్పణంటు నందు
తెలిపెనందరికిని విశదమగునట్లు.

ఆ|| తల్లి గోద తనను దయచూడ కరుణతో
పాశురంబులన్ని తెలుగు లోన
వ్రాయ, టిటిడి వారు దానిని ప్రకటింప,
కనక దుర్గ పాడ, విస్తరిల్లె.

తే|| అనుదినంటున చీకటినండె లేచి
స్నానసంధ్యాది చకచక ముగిసినంక
తంగుతంగున గంట మోగించి తెలిపె
భగవదారాధన సమయ మయ్యె ననుచు.

తే|| శిష్ట నిష్ఠా వ్రతుండు స్వసాధనంటు
తాననుసరించి బోధించె తదితరులకు
అన్ని భాగ్యంటులన్ విద్యగొప్పదంచు
అదియలేకున్న తానధమాధమంచు

తే|| ఆదరించె తన నెల నాదరము తోడ
సప్తసంతానమున్న సహృదయ తోడ
ఆశ్రయంటు జూపె ఇతరులకు కూడ
వారవటువులకును అన్యవర్గములకు.

తే|| తమసుఖంటులు కోరికలన్ త్యజించి
అందరి చదువులకు వెనుకాడకుండ
వారివారి పెచ్చాలు వారడిగినంత
కాని వ్యర్థంటు కాక లెక్కించి నిచ్చె.

తే|| కాదది గృహంటు నదియొక నాశ్రమంటు
తెచ్చునోకడప చెరువు నీరు దినదినంటు
బావి నీళ్ల పనికి కొంతమంది యుండ
ఆవు పాలు పిండ నోకడు గడ్డి పెట్ట.

తే|| చంటి పిల్ల యొకటి సదా చంక నుండ
వంటలన్ని మరియు పిండివంటలన్ని
ఎల్లరకును నాతల్లి చేసె, సహనముగ
గంటగొట్టక ముందె యారాధనకును.

తే|| ఇచ్చె సర్వులకును తిరిగివ్వమనకుండ
ఒక్క పైస నైన పరులనుంచి యైన
దేహీ యని బిక్షకై మాధవుండు కూడ
ఎంతనెంత వాడింతయైనాడటంచు.

తే|| భాగవతసేవతో తనజీవనంటు
ఆ మహాలక్ష్మి జయలక్ష్మి పత్నితోడ
తాను నమ్మినదే చెప్పెనందరికిని
ఎల్లరకు బోధజేసె తాననుసరించి.

తే|| పూర్వజన్మ పుణ్యఫలంటు వలన గాదె
లభ్యమాయెను మాకు నీ తల్లి తండ్రి
ఆంధ్రగీర్వాణ భారతీ పుత్రుడతడు
సకల కళ్యాణ జయలక్ష్మి తల్లి యామె.

***

సాష్టాంగ ప్రణామములతో సమర్పించు, సదానంద

INTRODUCTION

The Alwars are well known to everybody. Among them was born the divine incarnation of Bhu Devi, as Andal, or Goda Devi. Her work *Tiruppavai* is widely sung in temples, particularly in Vaishnava Temples in the South. Shree Kuntimaddi Seshasarma has written an excellent commentary called Melinomu in Telugu, published by Tirupati Tirumala Devasthanam (TTD). He was a well-known pundit and author of many books in Telugu and Sanskrit, several of which were published by TTD. To make his work available to all, his son, Shri Sadananda, with the help of his siblings, translated this work into English while keeping many of the Telugu poems intact.

Every word in the Tiruppavai has a deeper meaning, and Shree Sarmaji brings this out for us. The underlying theme of the Tiruppavai is a complete surrender of oneself to Lord Narayana through Saranagati or prapatti that Vishishtadvaita advocates. Shree Sarmaji establishes this using various pramanas from smriti and shruti texts. In this work, Pothana Bhagavatam is quoted extensively.

The Tiruppavai can be divided into mainly three sections. In the first section, Andal Devi decides to perform the Margasira-ritual with her fellow milkmaids. Now the question arises, why should one always worship

Narayana? Shree Seshasarma says, **"Only Shreeman Narayana can bless a Jeeva to reach His abode. Hence Shree Goda Devi says, 'Narayanane namakke parai tharuvaan.' Lord Narayana alone can fulfill our desires. Hence, we must serve Him only".** But why Narayana alone can provide the final stage? To answer this question, Shree Seshasarma says, **"Those who surrender to other Gods such as Brahma, Shiva, etc. will gain only very little, and that too momentary happiness. It is because their powers are limited. Hence, one cannot get liberated from this samsara by surrendering to them"** He quotes Lord Krishna's statement – mamevaye prapadyanti maayaam itaam tarantiti, **only by surrendering to Me one can cross this ocean of maayaa.** Since the worship of Narayana is a must to gain moksha, Shri Adal invites everybody to join her in the prayer. Shree Sarmaji reveals, **"One should not enjoy sweets alone, mainly when there are others around. Is there anything sweeter than the Hari-Bhajan? Hence it should be shared with others".** it might appear as though the worship of Hari is expensive and not everyone can afford it. Shree Sarmaji says that is not true. Why? He says, **"Offering with total devotion even a handful of food is sufficient instead of offering a big pot full of donkey's milk without devotion. God does not look at the price and quantity of things one offers. He only takes the devotion and leaves the rest.** Hence Krishna says in Geeta, पत्रं पुष्पं फलं तोयं यो मे भक्त्या प्रयच्छति ।तदहं भक्त्युपहृतमश्नामि प्रयतात्मनः **Bhagavan says that whoever offers me even a leaf, a flower, a fruit, or even some water, with supreme** devotion, I enjoy those very much. What I look for is devotion rather than the things that are offered".

Shree Sarmaji brings about an interesting episode from Ramayanam. He says," **Seeta's story tells us that even if one gets far removed from the Lord, a Jeeva can unite back with the Lord by surrendering completely. The key is complete surrender to the Lord by manasaa, vaachaa, karmanaa – by mind, speech, and action. Even Seeta let Rama go far away from her by rejecting the wise advice of Lakshmana. Also, by rebuking the Lord's devoted servant for not listening to her demands, she got trapped. She had to spend her time far away from the Lord. Just as Seeta got deluded by looking at the fascinating deer, a Jeeva gets deluded, forgets the Lord, and gets bound to the fascinating world of plurality and the world, life after life".** Through this comparison, Shree Sarmaji is compassionately persuading all humans to fix their minds on the Lord without being attracted and deluded by various material pleasures. What better advice can one give?

Now, who is eligible for the worship of Narayana? Can everyone worship him? Is everyone eligible for the highest abode? To answer all this questions the shree Saramaji uses a single sloka from Gita " मां हि पार्थ व्यपाश्रित्य येऽपि स्युः पापयोनयः |स्त्रियो वैश्यास्तथा शूद्रास्तेऽपि यान्ति परां गतिम् "**All those who take refuge in Me, whatever their birth, race, gender, or caste, even those whom society scorns, will attain the supreme destination".** Hence no further doubts need to be encouraged here.

However, to attain Mukthi, one must burn away all his karmas. We have accumulated karmas from many births in the past, and by God's grace now born as human beings with discriminative intellect. How can we attain mukthi then? Hence Shree Sarmaji explains what Goda Devis says. **"Pray to Damodara with a pure mind, speech, and actions – manasaa, vaachaa, karmanaa. Using the mind, meditate on him, using the tongue to sing His glories, and with hands worship Him with beautiful flowers. If we do that as she says, all our sanchita and aagaami karmas will get burned away completely like big cotton hill with a small spark from fire"**. The remaining Prarabdha karma has to be experienced but can be reduced through the lord's grace. Hence Shree Sarmaji answers all the questions and establishes that the surrender to Narayana will become the fulfilment of life itself. His commentary reminds us of the Lord's assurance in Gita "मामेकं शरणं व्रज" take refuge in me and "मा शुच:" do not fear.

Shree Sharmaji brings up an interesting note. What differentiates between an animal and a human being?" **To perform the four purusharthas (dharma, artha, kaama, and moksha), the Lord has provided the needed Jnanendriyas and karmendriyas for human beings",** these are not present for the animals. But knowing that only the last purushartha is permanent, he should aim for that alone. But what is this "surrender" to Hari? What should one do? Should he give up daily duties? No. Shree Sarmaji explains **"Goda Devi teaches all of us in** a way that we should get up every day before sunrise and, after cleaning ourselves, perform the daily duties with the feeling that all these activities become rituals if we keep our minds on the Lord and, if possible, keep chanting his name, while performing the routine physical activities". What is the fruit of these actions? "By singing the glories of the Lord or chanting the name of the Lord, reminding ourselves that even the body is functioning only because of His grace, our mind gets purified. It also prevents the mind from running into unnecessary self-centered activities and keeps the mind peaceful and serene. By His grace, the six enemies that bother the mind constantly, desire, anger, greediness, delusion, pride, and evilness – the six enemies will not enter our mind, thereby keeping it ready to serve the Lord, who is expressing Himself as the entire universe". Hence in the first section itself, Shree Sarmaji resolves all the queries that might arise in our minds.

In the second section, Devi is calling upon various Milkmaids to attend the ritual. But some of them are still sleeping. Hence, she wakes them up with harsh words. But how should the milkmaids sleeping be interpreted? Why does Devi use such harsh words? Shree Saramji explains this in this section. Initially, comes the question, is acquiring wealth wrong? Is experiencing bliss through them wrong? To answer this question Shree Sarmaji brings about the answer "One must experience the pleasures and comforts to the degree that Lord has bestowed on us. However, desperately depending on wealth or

luxuries will make us become a slave to them. One should experience these as though it is His prasad or gift for us, with a reverential attitude, and share these with those who are less fortunate".

And the fact that wealth should be acquired through Dharma alone is also implied here. Hence this attitude must be maintained. Here "sleeping" of the milkmaids is explained by Shree Sarmaji to be Tamo Guna. There are many other traits that come under the umbrella of Tamo guna. The idea here is that these Gunas must be eliminated through bhakti and have to be replaced with Sattva Gunas. Now the experience of bliss is due to the Prarabdha karma of the Jeeva, but the Paramatma who is the antaryamin never gets affected due to it. To explain how Shree Sarmaji takes the Sruthi reference here. He quotes the Mundaka Upanishad," **Two birds with brilliant wings are sitting friendly on the same tree. One eats and enjoys the sweet leaves of the Pippala tree, while the other observes the eating bird without indulging itself in eating. Here the body is picturized as a tree. The two birds correspond to one Jeeva and the other paramaatma. They are sitting friendly on the same tree or in the same body. Among them, Jeeva enjoys the fruits of his actions without thinking of others. The other one, Paramatma, is silently observing Jeeva enjoying the fruits. Thus Paramatma remains only as a sakshi (witness) when Jeevatma experiences the results of his own willful actions".**

We see that Devi uses harsh words to wake up the milkmaids. Why is this so? Sarmaji clarifies this doubt. It is to motivate us to start worshipping the lord without any delay or postponement. Why should we do that? Sharmaji explains **"Both lotuses and lilies have a short life. As though they are teaching us that life is very short, and any apparent glory is only short-lived. The water lilies were blooming the whole night and are now fading away in the morning. On the other hand, while closing their petals in the night, the lotuses begin to bloom again once morning comes. The water lilies are teaching us that once we have secured a birth in this human form, during our short life, we should not be going for external material things and temporary sense pleasures. Instead, we should strive for eternal, everlasting happiness that we can secure with the grace of God".** Hence this is the purport of the Harsh words Devi uses to wake us up.

In the third section, the milkmaids reach the fort of the Lord. Now to wake Him up they recite various stotras. The various descriptions of the fort and other venues are given. But the implied meanings of these things are very subtle and cannot be understood by everyone upon reading it at first. Shree Sarmaji brings out the implied meanings of these things. Shree Sarmaji says **"Devotees should go near God only after receiving a blessing from Acharya. In addition, when we go to the temple, we must project a devotional attitude in terms of dress, speech, and mental attitude – manasa-vaachaa- karmanaa. The**

Lord recognizes the attitude with which the devotee is approaching Him. The dress and the speech should reflect the attitude of service and surrender to Lord Vishnu".

Among the stotras made by the milkmaids, there is philosophy embedded in them. Upon reaching the Lord they make various prayers for him to have his darshan. But it appears as though he is not coming out, after all, is it that easy to get the vision of the supreme?

Hence their prayer **"We know the absolute truth of who you are and who we are. We know that you are the master, and we are your property. You are eternal, and we are part of you. You have said in Geeta, that we are part of you"**. And they continue by **"Since we are part of you and belong to you, is it not your responsibility to protect us? Does anyone have to remind you of this?"**, then the bold proclamation is made" **If you do not protect your property, who will be looser"?** After all, doesn't a devotee have such liberty with his beloved Lord? After all such prayers and the stotras, it has to be admitted that the Lord's greatness can never be captured by words and prayers. Hence Shree Sarmaji quotes Shri Yamunacharya to prove this point **"When Vedas and Gods, Brahma, Rudra, Sanaka Sanada, etc., could not describe you, who are we to describe and praise?"**

Among various impedances to mukthi, Ahamkara or the feeling of "I"ness is the hardest to overcome. Shree Sarmaji says **"Hence the feelings of I-ness (ahankara or** ego) and my-ness (mamakara or notion that all this is mine) only contribute to one's degradation as they are not real. Any individual or Jeeva himself belongs to Him. Hence it is better to surrender to His holy feet as that is where a Jeeva belongs. Thus, on those who recognize the above facts and surrender completely, He pours out His compassion, which can be seen by His compassionate looks".

Finally, the supreme lord wakes up and comes to give his darshan. Why won't the lord come when his devotees call him affectionately? Didn't he come running when Gajendra called upon him? Didn't he protect Draupadi when she called him? Didn't he protect his friend Arjuna throughout Mahabharata? Hence let there not be any doubt with regard to this. The lord's description when he comes out is given beautifully. **"In the rainy season, King Lion, while staying inside his cave and sleeping fearlessly, after hearing the thunder and getting up irritated due to the sound, angry and ferocious for getting disturbed from a sound sleep, came out of the cave to punish the culprit, not finding anyone there who made the noise, shook his head spread his hair, stretched himself, and went out to ignoring little animals here and there and claiming his majestic thrown, which is at a high level. In the same way, Gopicas are picturizing Lord Krishna's situation"**.

Shree Sarmaji says that the lord shouldn't be angry with the devotees for coming at an inappropriate time. Aren't we his kids? Can there be an inappropriate time for a child to see his beloved father? The liberty Gopikas have with the lord is only due to their immense devotion. **"Gopika girls who were intensely enjoying the company of Krishna, His temporary absence, even for a few hours, became intolerable".** Such was their devotion. The Gopikas only appear as though they are asking for boons with regard to the ritual. While in reality, it's only a pretext to be with their beloved lord. Why? Shree Sarmaji says **"When the Lord is there to protect and take care of the whole welfare of the devotees, it appears to be silly to go and ask Him to give small, silly material things in life. Does it not show ignorance on the part of the Seekers? Hence the devotees who are knowledgeable seekers do not ask for worldly sense objects but only for the eternal happiness of being associated with Him".**

An objection might be raised that isn't moksha also a desire? Isn't the devotee selfish in this regard? No, says Shree Sarmaji, **"Even our request for moksha is only to serve your holy feet. That we feel is essential for all Jeevas. This service can be done there in the highest abode or here itself remaining on this earth. It is the same. Hence Kulashekhara Alwar prays that all he wants is that he be blessed to have devotion towards him life after life".**

In summary, Shree Sarmaji deals with various topics while explaining the seemingly simple verses of the Thiruppavai. The various topics of bhakti, moksha, sharanagati, nature of Paramatma, etc. have been discussed while giving strong supporting evidence from shruti, smriti, and my personal favorite Pothana Bhagavatam. For any devotee, this work will be as sweet as nectar as it contains the greatness of the lord as well as his supreme nature.

– Namo Narayana

Kaushik Cevendra

Hyderabad

October 10, 2022

PASURAM 1

....

Introduction:

After the Kaliyuga started, for the upliftment of Dharma, many great saints were born in South India. Among them, the most famous are two Alvars (from the Srivaishnava tradition), referring to Goddess Andal and her father, Shree Vishnuchitta. There are twelve Alvars in the Srivaishnava tradition, and all are considered divine beings.

भूतम् सरस्च महदाह्वय भट्टनाथ
श्री भक्तिसार कुलशेखर योगिवाहान्,
भक्तान्घ्रिरेणु परकाल यतीद्रमिश्रान्
श्रीमत्परान्कुशमुनिम् प्रणतोस्मि नित्यम्.

In this above sloka, all the twelve great devotees were mentioned. We can recognize in the above sloka, for example, Shree Kulashekhara Alvar, who was the composer of the famous 'Mukundamaala.' The divine episodes of these Alvars have been beautifully described in the book 'Paramayogi Vilasam' composed by Tallapaka Tiruvengalanatha (also called Chinanna), the grandson of Annamacharya. The work deals with the glorious lives of the Alvars and Acharyas, Nathamuni, Yamuna, and Ramanujaacharya.

Among these 12 Alvars, only one is the divine lady, who is none other than Shree Goda Devi. It was her story only that the Vijayanagara Emperor, Sri Krishnadeva Raya, wrote as the central theme in his famous book in Telugu Literature, 'Amukta Maalyada,' also called 'Vishnuchitteeyam' since it contains the story of Alvar Vishnuchitta.

Vishnuchitaa is well known also as Priyaalvaar or Bhattanatha. He was born in Kaliyuga, 47th year named as Krodha, Mithuna month, Sukla paksha (bright moon-phase), star Swaatee, Ekadashi day, Sunday. He is considered as the Garuda amsha (incarnation of Garuda). He was born in Purasphuda Brahmin family of Shree Padmaiyaar-Mukundaacharya. From childhood, he was very much devotedly serving the Lord in the divine abode of Shree Velliputtur, where Lord Krishna is on the farm of Vatapatrashaayi (like a baby lying on a banyan leaf, with a toe-finger in his mouth).

One day, the Bhattanatha family found a baby girl near Tulasi plants. It was Kaliyuga, 48th year named Nala, karkataka month, Chaturdashi day, Tuesday, star Pubba. The baby was considered to be the incarnation of Bhuudevi. The family adopted the girl and raised her with all love and care. She is the one who became later as Shree Goda Devi.

The girl bloomed day by day and grew up as a divine child with an intense devotion to the Lord. She used to wear it every day unnoticed, the garland intended as a prayer for the Lord in the temple. After wearing the garland, she used to look at her beauty with the garland in the mirror and enjoy every pose with utmost happiness while looking at her image from every conceivable angle. After enjoying herself wearing that garland, she used to put it back carefully in the original basket.

One day, her father noticed that. While getting angry with her, he felt it would be a sin to offer that used garland to the Lord. Hence on that day, the Lord in the temple had no Garland. On that night, during his dream, the Lord appeared to Bhattanatha (who is affectionately called Vishnuchitta -that is, whose mind is constantly dwelling on the Lord Vishnu), and informed him that 'she is the incarnation of Bhuudevi. Because of her only wearing, the garland has acquired that divine smell. It will be My pleasure to ware that garland that she wore. Hence, please offer Me the garland only after she decorated herself with that'. For that reason, only she got the name 'Amukta Maalyada,' the one who wore the garland before it was offered.

It is her composition only that is being called as 'Tiruppavai,' that is being chanted every day in all temples of the Lord Vishnu, in South India, as part of morning Suprabhatam ritual. This present commentary in Telugu 'Melinomu' is based on Shree Goda Devi's Tiruppavai composition.

నీలచన్గొండ శిఖరాల నిద్రముస్తు,
కృష్ణు మేల్కొల్పి, వేదనిర్ణీత తత్వ
రత్వమెటిగించి భుక్తహోరమున గట్టి
బలిమి భోగించు గోదకు వందనములు.

(the above sloka is my father's composition in Telugu). Before, in Repalle, the young milkmaids played with the young Krishna. They were told not to do so by their elders. However, the milkmaids became desperate and were longing to play with the young, charming Krishna.

It so happened then that the village ended up having a severe drought. To relieve the people's suffering, the village elders only instructed the milkmaids to perform the Margasira-ritual under the leadership of Lord Krishna. The milkmaids were very happy, thinking that under this pretext, they got an excellent opportunity to be very close to Lord Krishna and enjoy his divine presence. Hence, they performed the ritual with great enthusiasm, getting up very early in the morning, despite the severe cold (December-January season).

In the same way, Shree Goda Devi, imagining that she is the leader of the milkmaids, took the role of prompting all the village young girls to join her in the performance of the Margasira-ritual, to sing the morning Suprabhatam for the Lord, to fulfill their longing desires to be intimately close to the Lord. With that image in mind, she composed this Tiruppavai in Tamil, 30 paasurams, to cover the ritual for the whole month of Margasira.

In the Tiruppavai, the theme is centered on the essential duties that must be performed for being blessed with human birth. Dharma, artha, kaama, and moksha constitute the four purushaarthaas for all beings, both males and females. Purushaarthaas are those actions that must be performed to fulfill the very purpose of human life. Otherwise, Life becomes a waste.

The gross external body belongs to Prakriti. It is formed by the five gross elements constituting the Prakriti. The gross bodies that we see are of divergent nature. The souls, which are called Jeevas, take birth in different types of bodies, starting from those of insects, bees, birds, cows, tigers, human beings, etc. These souls or Jeevas are of atomic size (anu pramaanam), based on the Vishishtadvaita-doctrine. Therefore, souls cannot be seen. The Jeeves take birth, taking different but suitable bodies depending on their past karmas. They undergo the cycles of births and deaths continuously and, in the process, undergo suffering, called samsara. After many births, they are blessed to be borne as human beings due to their accumulated good fortune. In human birth alone, they have a discriminative intellect. In addition, they are well equipped with the karmendriyas, or organs of action, and jnaanedriyas, instruments for knowledge.

Along with these, they can also acquire a discriminative intellect, Viveka, to know what is dharma and adharma. By using such a discriminative faculty, one can evolve into higher beings (devatas, etc.) or even gain the most exalted state of liberation or moksha that frees him from this cycle of births and deaths. Moksha is the ultimate purushaartha and forms the essential goal of human life, fulfilling the very purpose of human birth.

To gain moksha, jnaana, karma, and bhakti yogas form the means. However, all these yogas involve significant human efforts. One has to have prerequisites to be qualified for each. Only one in hundreds or one in cores can achieve these. On the other hand, the path of 'Prapatti' is very easy for everyone, says Shree Ramanuja, and it is guaranteed to give the end result. In essence, that path of 'Prapatti' is being described in these Tiruppavai pasurams, by Shree Goda Devi to help those who want to attain the moksha in this Life itself.

Pasuram: 1

Introduction: Shree Goda Devi is calling her milkmaid friends to come to perform the Margasira-ritual.

மார்கழித் திங்கள் மதி நிறைந்த நன்னாளால்
    நீராட போதுவீர் போதுமினோ நேரிழையீர்
சீர் மல்கும் ஆய்ப்பாடிச் செல்வச் சிறுமீர்காள்
    கூர் வேல் கொடுந்தொழிலன் நந்தகோபன் குமரன்
ஏரார்ந்த கண்ணி யசோதை இளஞ்சிங்கம்
    கார்மேனிச் செங்கண் கதிர் மதியம் போல் முகத்தான்
நாராயணனே நமக்கே பறை தருவான்
    பாரோர் புகழப் படிந்து ஏல் ஓர் எம்பாவாய்.

Maargazhi thingal madhi niraindha nannaalaal

Neeraadap podhuveer podhumino naerizhaiyeer

Seer malgum aayppaadich chelvach chirumeergaal

Koorvael kodundhozhilan nandhagopan kumaran…

Aeraarndha kanni yasodhai ilam singam

Kaar maeni sengan kadhir madhiyam pol mugathaan

Naarayananae namakkae parai tharuvaan

Paaror pugazhap padindhaelor empaavaay (1)

We skip the word-by-word meaning here that my father provided in his book, Melinomu.

Explanation: 'यम् प्राप्य न निवर्तन्ते तत् धाम परमम् मम' (Geeta 8:21), meaning those who after reaching the abode of Bhagavan, do not return to this samsara. They are essentially free from the cycle of birth and death, having reached the ultimate abode, the Vaikunta. Lord Narayana mentioned that His supreme abode, Vaikunta, is the highest of the three levels of places. (पादोऽस्य विस्वाभूतानि त्रिपादस्य अमृतम् दिवी, from the Purusha suuktam). Only Shreeman Narayana can bless a Jeeva to reach His abode. Hence Shree Goda Devi says, '*Narayanane namakke parai tharuvaan.*' Lord Narayana alone can fulfill our desires. Hence, we must serve Him only. He is called Narayana, meaning one who fulfills our desires.

Epistemologically, naaram means a group of naras or human beings. For them, aayanam or shelter, or gati or goal, as well as the protector, controller, is Narayana. Hence, we must seek his shelter or protection only, says Goda Devi.

This samsara, this Prakruti, or this maayaa is due to His Prakriti-Shakti or maayaa-shakti. A human can't cross over on his own. Only by His grace can one overcome this maayaa.

'दैवीम् येषा गुणमयी मम माया दुरत्यया,
मामेवये प्रपद्यन्ते मायामेताम् तरंति ते.'
(Geeta 7:14)

Those who surrender to other Gods such as Brahma, Shiva, etc. will gain only very little, and that too momentary happiness. It is because their powers are limited. Hence, one cannot get liberated from this samsara by surrendering to them.

Geeta further says, in support:

कामैस्तै स्तैर्हत ज्ञानाः प्रपद्य्नतेऽन्यदेवताः
तम् तम् नियम मास्थाय प्रकृत्या नियतान् स्वया।
यो यो याम् याम् तनुम् भक्तः श्रद्धयार्चितुमिच्छति।
तस्य तस्याचलाम् श्रद्धाम् तामेव विदधाम्यहम्॥

स तया श्रद्धया युक्तस्तस्याराधन मीहते
लभते च ततः कामान् मयैव विहितान् हितान्।

अन्तवत्तु फलम् तेषाम् तद्भवत्यल्प मेधसाम्।
(Geeta 23-7:20)

Hence, Narayana alone can give the supreme state, says Shree Goda Devi. Therefore, we must only worship Him by glorifying Him and serving Him.

Q. Who are those that Narayana blesses and fulfills their desires? Or How can we deserve His blessings?

After spending many lives in the form of insects, bees, animals, and birds, we have finally qualified to have these human bodies. Scriptures say, 'यस्यात्मा शरीरम्,' we are part of the body of Bhagavan.

ममैवांशो जीवलोके जीव भूतस्सनातनः, says Geeta (15:7). We are part of Him. He is sheshi, independent, and we are sheshulam, dependent on Him.

In essence, we are part of Him. We are eternally related to Him as part of His body. This is shown in the Virat Swaruupam of the Lord in the 11th Ch. of Geeta. Hence, by taking shelter in Him only, our desires will get fulfilled.

Potana Bhagavatam (in Telugu) says:

కలలోనన్ దను ముస్నెఱుంగని మహాకష్టాత్ముడై నట్టి దుర్బలు డాపత్సమయంటునన్ నిజపదాబ్జాతంబు ఉల్లంటులో(దలపన్నంతన మెచ్చి యార్తి హారు(డై తన్నెన నిచ్చున్ సుని శ్చల భక్తిన్ భజియించు వారికిడడే సంపద్విశేషోన్నతుల్.

Thus, for those who worship Him with full devotion, He will definitely fulfill their desires.

Therefore, Oh! My dear fellow milkmaids, please come and join me in His worship, says Shree Goda Devi.

As a general rule, the service will be very effective and joyful instead of doing alone when we do it together with like-minded friends. As the saying goes, 'एकः तपः, द्विरध्यायी', for tapas or meditation, one has to do alone. The presence of others will cause a disturbance. For studies, it is better to have two people studying together. The presence of the second provides extra support. If there are too many people, then it becomes chaos. For doing service to Lord Hari, or for Bhajan, it is better to have a manageable group. It provides a lot of enthusiasm and fulfillment in doing the Bhajans in a group.

One should not enjoy sweets alone, mainly when there are others around, as the saying goes, 'एकम् स्वादुन भुंजीत'. Also, Vidura neeti says (Telugu), 'విను మధురాహారంటులు గొనుటయు .. చనదొక్కనికిన్'. Is there anything sweeter than the Hari-Bhajan? Hence it should be shared with others.

हे जिह्वे रससारज्ञे सर्वदा मधुर प्रिये
नारायणाख्य पीयूषम् पिब जिह्वे निरंतरम्| (Vishnu Puranam)

The tongue always likes sweet. The above sloka says, 'Hence, Oh! Tongue! There is this sweetest nectar in the world. That is the name of Narayana. Drink that divine nectar and enjoy.'

There is a proverb, do not overindulge when something very tasty. If one overeats, even the nectar becomes poisonous. 'अजीर्णे भोजनम् विषम्' for the one who cannot digest, even the regular food becomes a poison. However, this does not apply to the divine nectar of Narayana Bhajan. One can drink as much as possible, and it will never become poisonous. Instead, it energies a person. If this divine nectar is shared with others, it becomes sweeter and even more enjoyable.

Bhajans to Bhagavan becomes a service to the community. The prayers become yaagam or yagna. 'యజ్ఞ దేవపూజాసంగతి, కరణ దానేషు' is the meaning for root 'yagna.' Here deva puja is mentioned first. Yagna – yaaga, words are derived from the root 'yaja.'

One who does not do the daily prayers to Gods (deva yagna) but enjoys worldly luxuries is considered a 'thief.' Gods are the ones who protect us from calamities, make sure that the rains come on time, the farmlands are productive, etc. Everything that we have is a gift from God. Not recognizing their service and enjoying it without doing their prayers will come under sin. Hence one must do prayers to the Gods who have given us plenty. By doing our daily prayers, we will not be committing sins. Hence Geeta says,

सह यज्ञाः प्रजास्सृष्ट्वा पुरोवाच प्रजापतिः
अनेन प्रसविष्यध्वम् एषवोऽस्तिवष्टकामधुक्‌|
(Geeta 1(3:10

Here prajaapati means Sri Mahaa Vishnu.

पतिम् विश्वस्यात्मेश्वरगम् शाश्वतगम् शिवमच्युतम्‌|
नारायणम् महाज्ञेयम् विश्वात्मानम् परायणम्‌||
(Narayana Suktam)

Thus, shruti says that only Narayana is the pati for vishvam or the universe. Vishvam includes everything that is sentient and insentient, and movables and immovables.

'पिताहमस्य जगतो माता धाता पितामहः,' and
further
'गतिर्भर्ता प्रभुस्साक्षी निवास शशरणम् सुहृत्,'
(Geeta 18-9:17)

Thus, I am the controller for the Universe, says Lord Krishna to Arjuna. Since He is the most compassionate and ever-present well-wisher of all, He makes the Jeevas who are in dormant form to become conscious, providing them with bodies and senses and making facilities for them to perform yagnaas for their evolution. Thus, He instructs them, 'Do these yagnas and enjoy the fruits and grow, by fulfilling your desires by performing appropriate yagnas.'

देवान् भावयतानेन ते देवा भावयन्तु वः
परस्परम् भावयतः श्रेयः परमवाप्स्यथ।
इष्टान् भोगान् हि वो देवा दास्यन्ते यज्ञभाविताः
तैर्दत्ता नप्रदायैभ्यो यो भुङ्क्ते स्तेन एव सः

यज्ञशिष्टाशिनः सन्तो मुच्यन्ते सर्वकिल्बिषैः
भुञ्जते ते त्वघम् पापा ये पचन्त्यात्मकारणात्।
(Geeta 13-3:11)

Thus, worship the Gods using these ingredients. The Gods, in turn, will protect you and provide what you need. In this way, by mutually satisfying, uplift yourselves while enjoying the fruits of your work.

While enjoying the abundant gifts from the Gods and not performing the deva-yagnas where one offers them with a reverential attitude, it is considered a thief. The yagna involves a cooperative action where the Jeeves contribute what they have got freely, and Devas, in return, bless them with plenty. Those who enjoy performing the yagna will not be incurring any sins. Krishna says one who cooks for himself and eats without sharing will incur sin. Cooking for oneself is similar to enjoying without acknowledging the help we received from the Gods.

The Gods are nothing but the ones who have paramaatma as their very soul. 'विश्वात्मानम् परायणम्' and again, 'वासुदेवात्म्कान्यायुः', 'क्षेत्रम् क्षेत्रज्ञ एव च' are shruti and smriti statements. It is said that for all Jeevas the soul is again paramaatma as antaryamin.

When one performs a puja to the body, it is, in a sense, prayer to the soul only since the body is just inert material. Similarly, praying to the Gods is only praying to their essential soul, Paramatma.

Hence, Gods such as Indra, etc., are the ones who provided the rains, which only means the Paramatma is being recognized via Indra, etc. In essence, prayer to the Gods has to be considered prayers to the Paramatma only. There is a well-known sloka that says,

आकाशात् पतितम् तोयम् यथा सागर गच्छति।
सर्वदेव नमस्कारम् केशवम् प्रतिगच्छति॥

The rains that fall from the sky ultimately reach the ocean. Similarly, all the salutations offered to different Gods ultimately reach Lord Narayana only. In addition, 'अहम् हि सर्व यग्नानाम् भोक्ता च प्रभुरेवच' is the statement of Bhagavan. Hence Deva yagna only means prayers to Bhagavan only.

द्रव्य यज्ञास्तपो यज्ञ योग यज्ञः तथापरे,
स्वाध्याय ज्ञान यज्ञास्च यतयः सम्शित व्रता।
(Geeta 4:28)

Thus, yagnaas are of different types. Whatever yagna is done, it becomes a prayer to Bhagavan only since He is the indweller of all Gods. Hence, one has to offer the best one has without struggling oneself, and the Bhagavan will accept His prayers. 'अनेन तृप्यताम् भगवान्नारायण:' with that feeling one has to do yagna to please the Lord.

One may be very poor, yet he has his body to offer. He has the senses to offer. They are enough. It counts not what you have but what you do with what you have. One who is very wealthy and offers the worth of his wealth is as good as the one who has nothing but offering with his full heart the chanting of the name of the Lord.

"नारायनेति मत्रोऽस्ति वागस्ति वशवर्तिनी
तथापि नरके घोरे पतन्तीत्येत दद्भुतम्" says Vishnupuranam.

There is Narayana mantram. For doing the Japa of Narayana, one is blessed with the tongue, which is entirely in one's control. But what is the use if it is not appropriately used to chant the most enchanting and most pleasurable Narayana Mantram? Without properly utilizing this God-given gift for humanity, misusing it and talking ill-will of others and using abusive language, wasting one's as well as others' time and money, cause self-destruction and others' downfall. They end up only in Naraka Loka, as to be expected. There is no wonder about that.

Hence Potana Bhagavatam (in Telugu) says:

చేతులారంగ శివుని బూజింప(డేని
నోరునొవ్వంగ హరికీర్తి నుడువ(డేని
దయయు సత్యంబులోనుగా(దలప(డేని
గలగనేటికి(దల్లుల కడుపుచేటు.

One who does not pray the auspicious (Shiva) and the one who is the remover of all our sins (Hari) that is the one who said, 'अहम् त्वा सर्वपापेभ्यो मोक्षयिष्यामि,' that Shreeman Narayana, his life is a waste. If one does not sing the divine glories of the Bhagavan, giving birth to such a person is a terrible waste, says Potana. (Following the Srivaishnava tradition, my father interprets Shivam as auspicious instead of Lord Shiva. The word also comes in the Vishunusahara naamaavali. Also, the Mandukya Up. Mantra 7 says, ' ....शान्तम् शिवम् अद्वैतम् चतुर्थम् मन्यंते स आत्मा स विज्ञेय:' where the meaning of Shivam again is auspicious, whether Potana intended that meaning or not is a separate issue).

Even though Shree Vyaasa Bhagavan wrote many puranaas, he was still restless. The Narada maharshi appeared in front of him and said,

'అంచితమైన ధర్మచయమంతయుచెప్పితి; వందులోన నిం
చింతుకగాని, విష్ణుకథలేర్పడ(జెప్పవు ధర్మముల్ ప్రపం
చించిన మెచ్చునే? గుణవిశేషము లెన్ని నగాక, నీకు నీ
కొంచెము వచ్చుటెల్ల హరి గోరి నుతింపమి నార్యపూజితా.

హరినామస్తుతి సేయు కావ్యము సువర్ణాంభోజ హంసావళి
సురుచి బ్రాజితమైన మానససరస్ఫూర్తిన్ వెలుంగొందు శ్రీ
హరినామస్తుతిలేని కావ్యము విచిత్రార్థాన్వితంబయ్యు శ్రీ
కరమైయుండద యోగ్యదుర్మళినవత్కాకోలగర్తాకృతిన్.

Thus, instructing him to compose Bhagavatam, which mainly contains Shree Hari's glorification.

Hence, Shree Goda Devi here only invites those who will join her in praising Lord Hari by saying *'poduminO'*, let us all together go to do His prayers.'

Even though all days are equal, as per the Hindu calendar, some days are considered auspicious due to the position of the stars.

"मासानाम् मार्गशीर्षोऽहम्" of all the months I am Margashira said the Lord in the Vibhuti Yoga. Hence Margashira is Hari swaruupam, and thus a very sacred month. In addition, on the full-moon night, it is very pleasing. Hence Shree Goda Devi calls, *'Maargazhi-th thingal madhiniraindha nannalal'*, in the early mornings, *'nerizhayeer'*, those wearing odd jewelry. Why qualify the jewelry as odd?

The rich people ware golden jewelry, and that is common and expected. There is no oddness in that. However, Shree Goda Devi says that if they are for decoration of oneself, are they real ornaments? –thus, she questions.

Bhartruhari says:

केयूराणि न भूषयन्ति पुरुषम् हारावतारोज्ज्वला:
न स्नानम् विलेपनम् नकुसुमम् नालङ्कृता मूर्धजा:

'భూషలుగావు మర్త్యులకు భూరి
మయాంగదతార హారములో'

These golden jewels are only a heavy burden to wear but not for one's real decoration. Then what are the real jewels that one should wear? For that Sumati composer says in Telugu,

"చేతులకు(దొడవు¹ దానము,
భూతలనాథునకు(దొడవు బొంకమి, ధరలో
నీతియె తొడవెవ్వారికి,
నాతికి మానంటు తొడవు నయముగ సుమతీ||
¹తొడవు = Jewels

In essence, he says, it is the proper conduct that is the real jewel for everyone. The 'Truth' is one great Jewel for everyone, and he shines brilliantly with that, rather than with any other jewel. Helping the needy with compassion, speaking the truth, ethical conduct, respect for the women, etc. are more precious ornaments to wear than the useless golden ornaments, which are just a heavy burden on the body, says Shree Goda Devi, in essence.

Furthermore, Potana says via Prahallada

కంజాక్షు నర్చించు కరములు కరములు
    శ్రీనాథు వర్ణించు జిహ్వా జిహ్వా
సురరక్షకుని జూచు చూడ్కులు చూడ్కులు
    శేషశాయికి మొక్కు శిరము శిరము
విష్ణునాకర్ణించు వీనులు వీనులు
    మధువైరి దవిలిన మనము మనము

భగవంతు వలగొను పదములు పదములు
పురుషోత్తముని మీది బుద్ధి బుద్ధి
దేవదేవుని జింతించు దినము దినము
చక్రహస్తుని(బ్రకటించు చదువు చదువు
కుంభినీధవు(జెప్పెడి గురుడు గురుడు
తండ్రి, హరి(జేరు మనియెడి తండ్రి తండ్రి.

On the contrary,

కంజాక్షునకు గాని కాయంబు కాయమే
పవన గుంభిత చర్మధక్క గాక
వైకుంతు బొగడని వక్త్రంబు వక్త్రమే
డమడమ ధ్వనితోడి ధక్కగాక
హరిపూజనము లేని హస్తంబు హస్తమే
తరుశాఖ నిర్మిత దర్విగాక
కమలేశు జూడని కన్నులు కన్నులే
తనుకుడ్యజాల రంధ్రములు గాక
చక్రిచింతలేని జన్మంబు జన్మమే
తరళ సలిల బుద్బుదంబు గాక
విష్ణుచింత లేని విబుధుండు విబుధుడే
పాదయుగముతోడి పశువుగాక.

And thus, the very purpose of our jnaanedriyaas and karmendriyaas are described by Potana. In essence, they are only meant for doing Hari puja and Hari Bhajan.

God has given these precious instruments only for doing His service, not for sense-enjoyments or glorifying oneself, which takes one further away from spiritual evolution.

Shree Goda Devi says her milkmaid friends are such extroverts that they care only for appealing external ornaments

Yet, she still calls them to purify themselves by taking a holy bath and then join her in the Hari Puja.

Any auspicious ritual is done only after taking a bath and purifying oneself. One can purify oneself by cleaning oneself in the flowing stream or river, outpouring rain, etc. while chanting the sacred mantras. Some people purify themselves by immersing in Holy rivers. Hence Shree Goda Devi is calling all her friends to join her in the Holy Marvashira-bath before entering the Sacred Temple for Hari Puja.

Hence, She says, *'Seermalgum aaipadi selvachirumeergal'*

All her friends are beautiful. 'यत्राकृति स्तत्र गुणाः' Where there is beauty there, the noble qualities also manifest. Hence all the milkmaids are cultured yet innocent village girls with well-behaved conduct. Their company is always a source of happiness.

Bad associations are like mud pots (or mad pots!). One should be far away from them as they break easily, and one cannot join them again to make the whole. On the other hand, the company of the good (sat sangham) is like the association with golden pots. They do not break easily. Even if they are dented by accidents, they can be repaired. Hence the association with them is desirable. Shree Goda

Devi wants to associate with them, and joining together wants to do service of Nanda kumaara (son of Nanda).

In addition, He is not a normal person. Hence Krishna says in Geeta,

यदा यदा हि धर्मस्य ग्लानि भवति भारत,
अभ्युत्थानमधर्मस्य तदात्मानम् सृजाम्यहम्‌।

परित्राणाय साधूनाम् विनाशाय च दुष्कृताम्‌,
धर्मसम्स्तापनार्थाय सम्भवामि युगे युगे।
(Geeta 8-4:7)

and thus, He incarnates every yuga to punish the wicked and to re-establish Dharma by uplifting the good. He further says,

अजोऽपि सन्नव्ययात्मा भूताना मीश्वरोऽपिसन्,
प्रकृतिम् स्वा मधिष्टाय सम्भवाम्यात्म मायया।
(Geeta 4:6)

He is the one who has no beginning and end (being infinite) and the controller of all phenomenal forces. He takes birth on His own accord. However, unlike other beings, His birth is not determined by His karmas. He is the creator, sustainer, and annihilator of the whole universe. 'जन्मादयस्य यतः' says Brahmasutra. He is the cause for jnama, sthiti and laya. The sutra is based on the Tai.Up mantra, यतोवा इमानि भूतानि जायन्ते...'

Thus, even though He is the leading cause, He assigns the creation part to Brahmaji, and the Laya part to Rudraji, while He takes care of maintenance. It is like assigning the portfolios while He remains as the Chief or the Prime. That Narayana only took birth as Lord Krishna. Hence Shree Goda Devi says,

'kaar mein-ch-chengan kadhir madhiyam pol mukathan'

He possesses a black body, bright red eyes, a face projecting divine beauty with the brightness of the Sun and Moon, etc.

Black symbolizes the tamasic guna, red the rajasic, and white brightness the sattvic guna. These are gunas or properties of Prakruti. He is beyond the prakruti while supporting it. He is bright and brilliant and beyond any three gunas. Hence,

न तत्र सूर्यो भाति, न चन्द्रतारकम्,
नेमा नक्षत्राणि भान्ति कुतोयमग्निः
तवेव भांतमनुभाति सर्वम्,
तस्यभासा सर्वमिदम् विभाति| (Kathopanishat)

Says Shruti. (This is chanted as Vedic Arati. That says while showing the flame that neither the Sun, nor the moon, nor the stars can illumine the Lord, how can this flame illumine Him, you are the light of lights and everything shines after you). To see Him, these external eyes are not sufficient. Hence in order to show His divine form, He blessed Arjuna with jnaana-chakshu or Wisdom-eyes.

न तु माम् शक्यसे द्रष्टु मनेनैव स्वचक्षुषा
'दिव्यम् ददामि ते चक्षुः पस्य मे योगमैश्वरम्|
(Geeta 11:8)

You cannot see my real form with your regular eyes, the product of the Prakriti. I will provide divyadrushti to see my true form, Oh! Arjuna! After seeing the Lord, in true form, Arjuna felt that his life is fulfilled. Arjuna said:

'तदेव मे दर्शय देव रूपम् प्रसीद देवेश जगन्निवास'
and
किरीटिनम् गदिनम् चक्रहस्तम् इच्छामि त्वाम् द्रष्टुम् तथैव,
तेनैव रूपेण चतुर्भुजेन सहस्रबाहो भव विश्वमूर्ते|
(Geeta 46-11:45)

Thus, he requested to show His previous form.

For humans born of Prakriti, the desires to possess the things made up of Prakriti are intense. Hence, Kalidasa says, सर्वस्वगन्धेषुविश्वसिति, everybody longs for only sense objects.

The Lord, who took in the human form to teach them the ultimate path, also behaves like a human being. Hence as though bound by Prakriti, He withholds His divine nature and exhibits Himself as a normal human being so that all others can easily approach Him without hesitation. However, that can also lead to misbeliefs for some; as Krishna says, 'अवजानन्ति माम् मूढाः मानुषीम्

तनुमाश्रितम्,' (Geeta 9:11) the ignorant think that I am a normal being and ignore my teachings.

In those days in the village, the disturbance created by Raakshaas, like Putana, etc., became intense. Hence even the peaceful and compassionate Nanda took to arms to protect the baby and became fearful. Hence Shree Goda Devi says, *Kooerval kodum thozhilam Nandagopan.* Seeing this, Yasoda says about his son, *'er aarndha kanni Yosadai ilam singam'.* He became a baby lion with beautiful but piercing eyes. It is said that even a baby lion can jump and smash an intoxicated elephant. In the same way, the baby Krishna like a little lion, jumped on to the big notorious nasty Rakshasaas like Putana, etc.

Hence, Shree Goda Devi calls her friends, saying, 'come all, let us all purify ourselves and then go to His divine abode to pray and glorify Him so that even the onlookers also get the benefit and enjoy the prayers.' Hence, she says, *'Paaror pugazha-p-padindul-el,'* come all join me. Let us all go by tying ourselves, and without any worries about the coldness of the weather and the water, take a bath. Without any hesitation, let us all dip ourselves in the running waters with sacred mantras to protect us.

Thus, Shree Goda Devi sings the first paasuram.

సిరిసంపదలు నగల్ చెలువమ్ము పరువమ్ము
    కొమరారు రేపల్లె కొమిరెలార,
పూర్ణచంద్రునితోడ(టొలుపొందు మార్గశి
    ర్షమునందు వేకువ జామునందు,

వాడిటల్లెము వేడి పనుల నందుని పుత్ర
కేసరి యా యశోదాసుతుండు,
*పుష్పసన్నిభమైన మోము కెందామరల్
మించు కన్నుల కట్టిమేనివాడు,
అఖిల మొసగును మనకు నారాయణుండు
లోకు లగ్గింప(టూని యో లోలనేత్ర
లార, యాతని పూజింప(గోరి నీర
మాడ(టోదము రండు రండతివలార|

* brilliance equal to the Sun and the Moon

PASURAM 2

Introduction:

Goda Devi explains the rules that must be followed for the ritual if one wants to do the ritual that she is doing.

வையத்து வாழ்வீர்காள்! நாமும் நம் பாவைக்குச்
  செய்யும் கிரிசைகள் கேளீரோ, பாற்கடலுள்
பையத் துயின்ற பரமனடி பாடி
  நெய்யுண்ணோம் பாலுண்ணோம் நாட்காலே நீராடி
மையிட்டு எழுதோம் மலரிட்டு நாம் முடியோம்
  செய்யாதன செய்யோம் தீக்குறளை சென்று ஓதோம்
ஐயமும் பிச்சையும் ஆந்தனையும் கைகாட்டி
  உய்யுமாறு எண்ணி உகந்து ஏல் ஓர் எம்பாவாய்

Vaiyaththu vaazhveergaal naamum nampaavaikkuch

Cheyyum kirisaigal kaeleero paarkadalul

Paiyath thuyinra paramanadi paadi

Neyyunnom paalunnom naatkaalae neeraadi

Maiyittu ezhudhom malarittu naam mudiyom

Seyyaadhana seyyom theekkuralaich chenrodhom

Aiyamum pichchaiyum aandhanaiyum kai kaatti

Uyyumaaru enni ugandhaelor empaavaay (2)

Meaning:

'Vaiyaththu vaazhveergaal' - Oh! Ladies, you are all blessed to be born as human beings for your speedy evolution! You are indeed blessed to be born here. In fact, there is no limit to your good fortunes. You are currently enjoying all the worldly pleasures. You must have done meritorious actions in the past. That is one of the reasons why you are all born in families with abundance. Now you are enjoying these endless pleasures. You are doubly fortunate to be born in Repalle at the same time when Shreeman Narayana has taken birth as Shree Krishna. That is not a simple accomplishment in your life. You are blessed, indeed. Now do not waste your life by enjoying these endless sense-pleasures.

These worldly pleasures are not permanent. By wasting your life on these enjoyments, you will waste away your hard-earned merits in past lives. Moreover, these sense pleasures are only binding, causing your slavery rather than giving you the everlasting happiness and liberation you intrinsically desire.

Hence Shree Harsha says, "पूर्वजन्मसुकृतव्ययलब्धाः संपदो विवद एव विमृष्टाः" - A similar statement was made in my Yatiraayeeyam book "సుకృతాయఫలంబు శ్రీ సిరులు వచ్చున్ తోఁవునవ్వానిపై నొక రాగంబు" – recognize that these worldly possessions are not permanent. The main goal in life is to inquire how to obtain the eternal, everlasting happiness that everyone strives for. Goda Devi says, do not get immersed in worldly pleasures and forget the very purpose of Life itself.

विबुध स्त्री सन्निधौ संयमः यत्कांक्षंति तपोभिः
अन्यमुनयः तस्मिन् तपस् अन्त्यमीः
(Shaakutalamu.)

Even after going to the heavens, the great sages do not desire these abundant sense pleasures. They desire only the supreme everlasting happiness and make all the efforts to achieve that. In the same way, Goda Devi advises the Gopika girls to give up the external sense pleasures and devote their time only to gain the supreme.

Do not say we are associated with Shree Krishna; what more do we want? Do not ask, now that we are close to Shree Krishna, why cannot we enjoy these sense pleasures, which are also challenging to get? Just as drinking Gange's water with devotion will help earnest seekers in destroying their sins and provide a means to go to the heavens, it does not mean that fishes, crabs, and other living entities in the Ganges water will go to heaven. One needs devotion and dedication to pursue the higher to get the desired results, and not otherwise.

"భక్తిగల్లు కూడు పట్టుడైనను చాలు కడవడైన నేమి ఖరము పాలు" – says Vemana. Offering with total devotion even a handful of food is sufficient instead of offering a big pot full of donkey's milk without devotion. God does not look at the price and quantity of things one offers. He only takes the devotion and leaves the rest. Hence Krishna says in Geeta,

"पत्रम् पुष्पम् फलम् तोयम् योमेभक्त्या प्रयच्छति।
तत् अहम् भक्त्युपहृतम् अश्नामि प्रयतास्मनः
(Geeta 9:26)

Bhagavan says that whoever offers me even a leaf, a flower, a fruit, or even some water, with supreme devotion, I enjoy those very much. What I look for is devotion rather than the things that are offered.

"దుస్సేనునుండి ద్రౌపది రక్షింప,
గ్రాహగళితమైన కరిని గావ
మూల్యమొసగి రేమి? మురహార! కేవల
భక్తి భజనలకును వశుడ వీవు." (My Sudhabinduvulu).

Lord (the one who killed the Mura demon) saved Doupadi from Dussaasana, and protected Gajendra from that crocodile. Did they offer vast sums of money to get their protection? Oh! Lord! You are only helping those who are entirely devoted to you. Or one can say that those who are entirely devoted to you get complete protection from you. 2

Hence Krishna says:

अनन्याश्चिंतयंतो मां ये जनाः पर्युपासते।
तेषां नित्याभियुक्तानाम् योगक्षेमं वहाम्यहम्॥
(Geeta 9:22)

Those who, without any other thoughts in mind, are wholly devoted to Me, I will take care of all their complete welfare (yoga and kshema) – That is My promise.

Indulging in the sense-pleasures for happiness is in no comparison to the happiness one gets with complete devotion to the supreme. Therefore, Goda Devi says, 'Oh! You All, who are wasting your time on sense pleasures, listen to you all. It is the time to give up all those which are temporary and bind you to worldly life. Instead, devote your minds to discovering the eternal inexhaustible happiness that you are entitled to. For that, you need to develop devotion toward the Lord.

In response to the question, 'What are you doing in this respect?' Goda Devi answers, "*naam, uyyumaareNNi*".

We, even though, like you, are born to a well-to-do family, recognize that all this wealth and pleasure are not permanent. We also understood that we are all incapable of following the rigorous paths of jnana, karma, and bhakti as discussed in Geeta, and recognize that the only resort for all of us is the path of Prappati or complete surrender as the ultimate path to secure eternal happiness. We also understood that without surrendering to the Lord and wasting precious time indulging in the sense-pleasures for happiness is like praying to the great wishing-tree (kalpataruvu) to give us some silly charcoal for use. Hence, we, *uyyumaareNNi*, discovered a method for a Jeeva to evolve.

Who is a Jeeva? If one asks, the answer is that Jeeva is one who is empowered to act by the blessing of the Lord. He is of the nature of consciousness-existence and the source of happiness. He, in essence, forms the part of the Lord.

Hence Geeta says, "ममैवांशो जीवलोके जीवभूतस्सनातनः" (Geeta:15:7). Thus Jeeva is part of the Lord. Hence, he possesses some of the attributes of the Lord. However, the Lord says,

'अपरेयमितस्त्वन्याम् प्रकृतिम् विद्धि मे पराम्, जीवभूताम् महाबाहो ययेदम् धार्यते जगत्"
(Geeta 7:5)

That Jeeva, even though being part of chit-swaruupam of the Lord, got deluded and hence got bound to the Prakruti or the world of plurality.

For example, Seeta got deluded by looking at the golden deer and, in the process, got separated from the Lord of the Supreme, Shree Ramachandra. By getting further away from the Lord, she suffered a lot in Lanka. Only with complete devotion to the Lord and spending all her time in meditation on Lord Rama, she finally got liberated from the clutches of the city of sense-pleasures. Hence a poet says Jeeva's life is similar to how Seeta's got separated and later reunited with Rama due to a temporary fascination of golden dear without realizing that it is just the outer delusory cover that fascinates when Jeeva fails to look deeper.

బంగరు జింకపైని గల భ్రాంతికి
లోగిన సీత రాముడన్
బంగరు దుప్పటినిని సనాతను
దవ్వుగ(జేసికొంట, నా
యంగన లంక బద్ధయయి ఆర్తి
నలంగి నిరంత చింతలన్

గ్రుంగెను గాదె, రామ విభు
నేముట బంధములన్ దొలంగదే.

Seeta's story tells us that even if one gets far removed from the Lord, a Jeeva can unite back with the Lord by surrendering completely. The key is complete surrender to the Lord by manasaa, vaachaa, karmanaa – by mind, speech, and action.

Even Seeta, let Rama go far away from her, by rejecting the wisdom advice of Lakshmana and also rebuking the Lord's devoted servant for not listening to her demands, she got trapped. She had to spend her time far away from the Lord. Hence the poet says,

రాముని దూరమంపినను ప్రాకృత
శంటర చర్మ కాంక్ష నా
రాముననుంగు సోదరుని రక్షణ
యుండిన నంత పుట్టునే
రామకు? గాన భాగవత రమ్య
దయారస మించకున్నచో(
టాములు సేరరావు భగవంతుని
సన్నిధి(జేర్చు నాతడే.

Just as Seeta got deluded by looking at the fascinating deer, a Jeeva gets deluded and forgets the Lord, gets bound to the fascinating world of plurality and the world, life after life. Of the millions of people, we see very few interested in getting out of this endless bondage to the sense-pleasures and trying to find fleeting happiness outside.

ప్రాకృతమాయ(దోగి పలు బాముల
నెత్తుచు, రాయి, గోయి వ
ల్మీకము మాను మక్షికము మీనము
నండజమున్ మృగమ్ము నై
ఆకలి కోర్చి, యొలి నరుడై
జనియించుచు నందు నెన్నియో
పొకల(తోవు నారకము నొందును
నాకము నాత్మ కర్మలన్. (from my Yatiraajeeyamu)

It says, in essence, that a Jeeva got caught in the Prakriti-Maaya (due to ignorance of his innate nature that he is part of the pure all-pervading sat-chit-ananda swaruupam of Brahman). He is born taking different bodies from trees to various animal forms and ultimately being born with a human body. Jeeva still goes through different lives and between heavens and hells, depending on his actions (karmas). It will continue forever unless he recognizes his role and completely surrenders to the Lord.

జ్ఞాతాజ్ఞాత పురాభవాSSరచిత
లోక శ్లాఘ్య కర్మావతీ
జ్ఞాతాSSచార్య దయాకరంచిత
కటాక్ష శ్రేణి, లక్ష్మీశు(గం
జాతాక్షుణ్ కనువిందుగా గన
సమర్చల్ చేయ(జింతింపగా(
జేతోవీథి(దలంపు పుట్టి హరి
సంసేవించు మోక్షార్థియై. (My Yatiraajeeyam)

In this human life, we now have opportunities to develop the required knowledge to surrender ourselves at the feet of the Lord. We have to make use of this opportunity that we are blessed with. Using this human body only, we can liberate ourselves from this endless chain of life and death. Without working to end our sufferings, if we still engage in the sense-pleasures and thus not only waste God-given opportunities but also accumulate more karmas that propel us to be born again and again, it will be a grave mistake. We may not get these opportunities again to evolve further. We do not know what life forms we will take if we misuse the current opportunities. Hence Goda Devi advises us to work for the upliftment of ourselves by surrendering at the feet of the Lord rather than indulging in sense-pleasures.

Moksha or liberation is given by 'Janardhana.' Hence one has to take shelter under Him only. Prakriti is under His control only; hence, to get liberated from the clutches of the Prakriti, surrendering to Him alone will help. Hence Krishna says, --....मम माया दुरत्यया, माम् एवये प्रपद्यंते मायम् एताम् तरंति ते| (Geeta 7:14). It is very difficult to cross this ocean of my maayaa by any self-effort. One can cross only by completely surrendering oneself to Me.

Even after acquiring the birth in the human form after millions of other lower forms of life, very few are interested in the liberation from the cycle of birth and death. Hence Krishna says, "मनुष्याणाम् सहस्रेषु.." (Geeta 7:3) of the thousands of people, very few are really interested in liberation. Many only waste their lives in acquiring wealth and enjoying it with their spouses and children, and in the end, they continue to suffer because of it. Even if the idea to evolve occasionally occurs, they postpone it to achieve it when they age. However, when old age hits, one will face innumerable problems of health, etc. As someone has said, 'many sacrifice their health to get wealth, and in the end, they have to sacrifice the wealth for the health.' Life is unpredictable. We do not know what will happen the next moment. Nothing is guaranteed. Hence it is better to work for solvation than postpone it to the future. "आयुः परिस्रवति भिन्न घटा दिवांभः" says Bhartruhari.

Water in a pot evaporates in time, similarly the life. Death can occur not only for the old but even for the young. That which is born has to die– जातस्यहि ध्रुवो मृत्युः – says Krishna. Hence death is inevitable, and we do not know when it will come. It can happen to anybody at any time.

బాలుని వృద్ధునేని, ధనవంతుని
పేదను గాని; మిత్తి, వా
చాలుని మౌని నేని, స్వవశం
బొ నరిచుకొనుం దెగించి, ని
ద్రాలుని జాగరూకుని పదస్థు
వనస్థు గృహస్థు నేని(, బ్రా
ల్మ లిన వాని నీరుజుని, మానక,
భోక్తను, పాయి, రంతనున్. (My Shantivilasamu)

When death is ready to engulf, it will be too late to think of doing something to evolve. Also, we do not know when it descends on us. What will we gain by repenting at that time what we did, and thinking about what we should have, could have, or would have done?

తనుధరు లెల్లవారలను తప్పక
  పోయెడి పారలౌకికాs
యనమున కర్మమై, ఇట నలభ్య
  ములౌ వసనాన్న పొన వా
హాన కరదీపికా తతుల నక్కట,
  యెుక్కటి గూడ నిల్చి సా
ధనము గడించు నూహా మది
  దట్టదు సుంతయు తిండిపోతుకున్. (My Shantivilaasamu)

Hence, one has to make every effort to gain liberation from samsara. It is better to get prepared. Hence Shankara says

भज गोविन्दं भज गोविन्दं
गोविन्दं भज मूढमते |
सम्प्राप्ते सन्निहिते काले
नहि नहि रक्षति डुक्रिङ्करणे

Therefore,

కాన నొనర్పగావలయు కార్యము
  లెప్పటి కప్పుడే సమీ
చీనము లైనచో, మరల(జేయుద
  మన్నను ఉద్బుదాభ మీ
మెను తిరమ్మె? రేపటికి మిత్తికి
  చిక్కక యుండు నంట కే

వానికి నెన్ని గుండెలు? కృపాజలధి
ననుగావు మెయ్యెడన్. (My Yatiraajeeyam)

Hence, we should start our prayers to Govind now instead of postponing to some future date. We do not know what will happen tomorrow. That is what Goda Devi says as 'uyyumaaru' (securing eternal happy life) as the life mission. That is what we have committed to do the ritual today and now. The Lord will bless us immensely for those who follow this path. Hence Oh! Ladies, please come and join us on this path and fulfill your life mission -says Goda Devi.

If you ask what the dos and don'ts for this ritual are, Goda Devi says, 'keshirO' – please listen. 'paal kaDaluL pai yettu parama naDippADi'.

The Lord, Shreeman Narayana, is waiting on his snake bed in a meditative posture to see when His disciple will come for their divine vision so that He can bless them.

One does not have to hesitate to wake up Lord from his divine meditative posture. His meditative sleep is not like our sleep which is of tamasic nature. It is called yoganidra or meditative sleep. Even though his external eyes appear closed and therefore appear that the external world is not visible, that is only from our viewpoint. He has a divine vision. He can see clearly the ins and outs of the entire world – not only this world but the higher and lower worlds. Anyone in this universe who is desperate and with intense longing calls Him, Oh! Govinda! Oh!

Narayana! Please help me! He responds immediately. That is His promise. Gajendra and Doupadi provide examples for us.

"Anybody calling me desperately for help or protection with full devotion so that I can immediately go and in a way to keep My promise to my devotees" with that in mind, Lord Narayana is contemplating with closed eyes and lying down on a snake-bed in the milky ocean. Unfortunately, He finds that most people only long for sense-enjoyments and are not interested in solvation.

One may say why He should wait for people to ask for help. Why cannot He help voluntarily without the Jeevas asking for it? Does a baby ask her mother to help? Does not the mother rush to help the baby and protect her without the baby asking for it?

That does not work. Most Jeeves not only do not ask for help but want to enjoy something else. That comes from the pressure of their karmas. Hence to be eligible for His help, one has to be devoted to Him and not to the sensory pleasure. Jeevas are given a choice to choose with the hope that they will make the right choice. Unfortunately, very few make the right choice. For that *purva janma samskaram* or evolved minds that can realize the uselessness of worldly pursuits and are ready to turn their minds towards Narayana are required. The creation is meant for individual evolution with the choice of action given. Hence even though the Lord is ever ready to help, the Jeeves have to ask for it. Even though He is all-knowing (sarvajna) and the most compassionate one and waiting when a Jeeva desperately asks for help, He comes to help only when Jeeva asks with total devotion, giving up all other efforts.

"हे कृष्णा! द्वारकावास पाहि! यादवनंदन|
इमामवस्थाम् संप्राप्ता मनाथाम् किमुपेक्षसे||

Thus, until Droupadi cried for help, asking Krishna to come and help after giving up all her self-efforts to protect herself, Krishna did not come, even though he is well-known as Pandavas protector. Hence Goda Devi says we must pray with devotion to save us. For that only, we will be doing this ritual while calling for Repalle girls to come for the prayer.

Hence it is our culture that any action or endeavor we undertake, we start with a prayer to the Lord to help us complete the undertaking successfully. If complete salvation is our goal, then complete surrender at his holy feet is the only recourse. If Lord has feet for us to surrender, He should have the rest of the body too. Hence prayer to form is the best since the mind can easily concentrate and surrender to Him.

One can pray to the formless God, but for fickle-minded people like us, it is challenging to keep the mind concentrated. Will the result be any different by praying to the formless one than to the one with the full form? If asked, the answer is no. In Ch. 12 of Geeta (Bhakti yoga), when Arjuna asked this question

एवम् सततयुक्ता ये भक्तास्त्वाम् पर्युपासते।
ये चाप्यक्षर मव्यक्तम् तेषाम् के योगवित्तमाः।
(Geeta 12:1)

"Those who pray this infinite auspicious form that you showed me and those that worship formless form, of the two who is supreme? Who will gain the final results faster?"

Krishna said it would not make any difference.

मय्यावेश्य मनो ये माम् नित्ययुक्ता उपासते।
श्रद्धया परयोपेताः तेमे युक्ततमा मताः॥
(Geeta 12:2-)

One who prays me in form with mind centered on Me, with complete devotion he is very dear to Me.

येत्वक्षरमनिर्देश्यम् अव्यक्तम् पर्युपासते।
सर्वत्रगमचिंत्यं च कूटस्थमचलम् ध्रुवम्॥
संनियम्येन्द्रिय ग्रामम् सर्वत्र समबुद्धयः
ते प्राप्नुवति मामेव सर्वभूतहिते रताः॥
(Geeta 4-12:3)

One who controls all the senses that generally run towards the sense-objects and contemplates on that which is beyond the comprehension of the mind and intellect, unchanging, eternal, formless, effortless all the time, with compassion to all beings with equanimity, they too reach Me. However

क्लेशोऽधिकतरस्तेशाम् अव्यक्तासक्तचेतसाम्।
अव्यक्ता हि गतिर्दुःखम् देहवद्भिरवाप्यते॥
(Geeta 12:5)

It is very difficult to constantly concentrate on the formless form for worldly-oriented people whose minds keep running toward external objects. It takes a lot of effort and struggles to accomplish this.

When one contemplates on the form or formless truth, the final result remains the same, then why should we pursue the most challenging path leaving the easy path? It would not make any sense, is it not? No intelligent person would want to pursue the difficult path leaving the easy one. Hence it is better to seek the auspicious delightful form of the Lord.

Sreeman Narayana only saved Gajendra, Shabari, JaTaayu, etc., by appearing in front of them and relieving their pains, is it not? Hence,

సగుణ నిర్గుణాది చర్చలు మన కేల
కులధనమ్ము మన ముకుందు డుండ
కనుల విందుగాగ గాంతు నాతని రూపు
జిహ్వ త్రుప్పుడుల్ల చేతు భజన| (My Sudhabinduvulu)

What is the point in arguing endlessly about which is better – worshipping formless God or form full God, when we are born in a culture of devotion to Lord Krishna? Let us devote our time to worshipping His divine form and chanting his divine name until we cannot chant anymore.

Hence, *'parama paDippaaDi'*, praising the lotus feet of Lord of the Universe at every step, let us start our ritual to worship Him, says Goda Devi.

Let us perform this ritual by getting up very early in the morning and glorifying the enchanting name of the Lord Narayana, *'naatkaale neeraaDi'*, taking a bath in the holy waters of the nearby stream before sunrise, without indulging ourselves *'nEyyiNNOm pAlNNOm'* in eating the delicious foods made up of ghee and the milk due to lingering desires in mind, says Goda Devi.

Here, ghee and milk are used as examples to designate all sense pleasures that the mind wants to indulge in all the time. They preoccupy the mind dissipating our energies. Those who discipline their minds by controlling them from running to these habitually and turning their attention to the highest truth, slowly get established in the highest truth. Krishna says the path is difficult but can be achieved slowly but steadily by constant practice and slowly giving up these temporary sense pleasures –'अभ्यासेनतु कौन्तेया वैराग्येणच गृह्यते' (Geeta 6:35). By constant practice (abhyaasa) and by slowly giving up sense-indulgence (vairagya) one can slowly control the mind. Hence, a disciplined mind is required; this is true if one wants to excel in life. It is more critical if one wants to reach the highest pinnacle of life.

It is indeed difficult for those whose minds are constantly indulged in the sense-pleasures. Hence Krishna says,

यदा सहरते चायम् कूर्मोऽगानीव सर्वशः।
इंद्रियाणीद्रियार्थेभ्यः तस्य प्रज्ञा प्रतिशिटता॥
(Geeta 2:58)

Just as the tortoise withdraws its limbs into its shell, a realized master withdraws his mind when encountering the sense-temptations.

Even after physically withdrawing the external sources of sense pleasures, if one still mentally indulges himself in those, he is only deceiving himself and perhaps others.

कर्मेंद्रियाणि संयम्य य आस्ते मनसा स्मरण्।
इंद्रियार्थान् विमूढात्मा मिथ्यचारस्स् उच्यते॥
(Geeta 3:6)

Hence a realized master always has his mind withdrawn from all these selfish desires but enjoys only by reveling in his mind the supreme reality. Hence Krishna says,

प्रजहाति यदाकामान् सर्वाण् पार्थ मनो गतान्।
आत्मन्येवात्मना तुष्टः स्थितप्रज्ञस्तदोच्यते।
(Geeta 2:55)

One who not only controlled senses from running to sense-object but also controlled his mind without mentally indulging in sense enjoyments and turned his attention entirely towards paramaatma is called sthitaprajna, says Lord Krishna. Even if we avoid the external sense objects, controlling the mind from internally indulging in sense enjoyments is very difficult indeed. Hence mental disciple has to be developed. One has to ensure that the mind does not run towards sense objects as long as one lives and turns his attention toward spiritual growth requires a disciplined mind. Only by controlling the mind one can slowly get rid of the innate desires and the associated vaasanaas to indulge in baser pleasures. Hence Krishna says,

विषया विनिवर्तंते निराहारस्य देहिनः।
रसवर्जम् रसोऽप्यस्य परम् दृष्ट्वा निवर्तते॥
(Geeta 2:59)

Senses like to have sense objects for their indulgence. Even if one removes the sense-objects, the longing to enjoy those will not go away easily. Hence, the only way to control them is to turn their attention to something higher, the highest being the Paramatma. Hence supreme devotion to the Lord also eliminates other mental dissipating desires and activities.

Thus, visualizing using the eyes as the most auspicious form of the Lord, engaging the tongue in divine prayers of the Lord, listening to the glories of the Lord with ears, etc., help the mind to get rid of all the lingering vaasanaas slowly and rapidly evolve in the spiritual path.

One who is addicted to playing cards does not remember even the darling wife waiting for him at home. Similarly, the mind fully engaged in the service of the Lord will not remember the sense objects. As Prahallada says, 'మందారమకరంద మాధుర్యమున దేలు మధుపంటు పోవునే మదనములకు' (Potana Bhagavatam) and

'అమృతరస మొల్కు విష్ణుపాదారవిందమందు మదిజేర్చి యొవ్వడన్యంటు గోరు' (from my Sudhabinduvulu)

One whose mind is absorbed in the enchanting divine feet of the Lord, why does he desire anything else? Hence, Kulashekara Alwar says in Mukundamala,

जिह्वे कीर्तय केशवम्, मुररिपुम् चेतो भजश्रीधरम्
पाणिद्वंद्व समर्चयाऽच्युत कथाश्रोत्रद्वयत्वम् शृणु।
कृष्णम् लोकय लोचनद्वय, हरेर्गच्छांघ्रि युग्मालयम्
जिघ्र घ्राण मुकुंदपादतुलसीम् मूर्धन्नमाधोक्षजम्॥

Sing the glories of Keshava with your tongue, do his bhajans and prayers with your hands, listen to his stories with your ears, see his divine form with your eyes, taste his blessed water and prostrate to him with total devotion. Thus use all your sense organs in his prayers.

Hence, Goda Devi says, during the prayer ritual, we do not think and desire any sense objects at all, '*neyyuNNOm paaluNNOm.*'

Even though we ladies like to decorate ourselves all the time, we have no more of these desires. We do not wish to waste our time now on these. The body full of filth will remain filthy even if we decorate ourselves externally. Hence there is no point in wasting time and money on that. It is better to spend that time doing His prayers.

That does not mean that we do not clean ourselves before prayer. We do not want to be looked at with disgust.

One can ask, 'when you are going to see Lord Krishna, why don't you go beautifully and attractively dressed and decorate your body with shining and glistering ornaments'? We know that the Lord only looks at inner beauty and not external superficial ornaments and decorations. He only looks for peaceful and serene minds filled with compassion, forgiveness, and good nature and conduct, not the external things you mentioned.

"sheyyadana sheyyOm – tIrukkuLai shenNOdam," We will not do any disgusting wrongful actions. Will not do any actions that hurt the devotees of the Lord. Will not utter words that hurt other beings, speak ill of others, lie to or abuse others – says Goda Devi.

With purified mind, speech, and actions, *"ayyayum picceyumaandnai kai kaaTTi"* after performing the worship of our teachers/Acaryas adequately and offering whatever we could with a reverential attitude to the needy, we undertake this worshiping ritual to the Lord.

"Oh! Noble ladies! You all come and join us in this ritual, following the rules and regulations laid down for its performance and worship Lord with us and *"ugalandu"*, happily enjoy. That is the only path available for us all, for our upliftment to reach the highest, *'uyyamaaRu,'* says Goda Devi.

For Jeeves, like insects caught in this whirlpool of samsara going round and round, life after life with no end in sight, the only easiest and guaranteed way of ending this suffering is to surrender completely at the divine feet of the Lord. Offering ourselves to the divine helps us attain our true nature, which involves serving the Lord as best as Jeevas can. That, in fact, is their final liberation involving becoming part of the *Viswaruupa Iswara*, enjoying His divine blessings all the time. That is the knowledge that we need to gain from our teachers. Without expecting any fruits of the actions, only desire to please the Lord to the best that one can, '*parama naDi ppaaDi*' and surrendering entirely at the divine feet of the Lord and praying and performing all the rituals that help the mind in surrendering the Lord constitute the essence of Karmayoga. Avoiding all the actions that take our minds away from the mind is also part of the discipline needed to accomplish this. Serving the devotees of the Lord in the best possible way and earning only what is required in a dharmic way all become ingredients in preparing our minds. With firm resolution that 'this is the highest path for the upliftment of our souls and with complete surrender to the divine will become the essence of sharanaagati.

Hence Goda Devi says in this second paasuram:

భౌతికభోగసౌభాగ్య భూషితలార,
పరమపదాప్తికి పథము గనుడు
నీరాడి వేకువ క్షీరోదశాయి ప

నీ రేజములను గీర్తించి మేము
చేసెడి వ్రతనిష్ఠ చెప్పెద చెలులార,
    కైకోము పాల్ నేయిగాని, మేము
పూలను గైసేయ(టోము కొప్పులయందు,
    కాటుక వెట్టము కన్నుగవకు
చేయ(గూడని చేతలు చేయటోము,
    పరులబాధించు పలుకులు పలక(టోము
చేతనయినంత యిత్తుము చేతులెత్తి
బీదలకు(టూజ్యపాదుల కాదరమున.

PASURAM 3

Introduction:

Goda Devi says that the performance of the ritual will be of benefit not only to her but also to many others.

ஓங்கி உலகளந்த உத்தமன் பேர் பாடி
    நாங்கள் நம்பாவைக்குச் சாற்றி நீராடினால்
தீங்கின்றி நாடெல்லாம் திங்கள் மும்மாரி பெய்து
    ஓங்கு பெருஞ் செந்நொலூடு கயல் உகள
பூங்குவளைப் போதில் பொறிவண்டு கண்படுப்ப
    தேங்காதே புக்கிருந்து சீர்த்த முலை பற்றி
வாங்கக் குடம் நிறைக்கும் வள்ளல் பெரும் பசுக்கள்
    நீங்காத செல்வம் நிறைந்து ஏல் ஓர் எம்பாவாய்.

Ongi ulagalandha uththaman paer paadi

Naangal nam paavaikkuch chaatri neeraadinaal

Theenginri naadellaam thingal mum maari peydhu

Ongu perum senn nel oodu kayalugalap

Poonguvalaip podhil pori vandu kan paduppath

Thaengaadhae pukkirundhu seerththa mulai patri-

Vaanga kudam niraikkum vallal perum pasukkal

Neengaadha selvam niraindhaelor embaavaay||

If we perform noble actions, it will benefit many people. It has been said if we perform a holy yajna for the benefit of society, it will give profound help to all the people protecting them from famine, etc., for nearly 12 years.

अन्नाद्भवंति भूतानि पर्जन्यादन्नसंभवः|
यज्ञाद्भवति पर्जन्यः यज्ञ कर्मसमुद्भवः" (Geeta 3:14)

By performing a yagna, rains will come, and due to rains, our land will become fertile, and in these fertile lands, varieties of grains can grow to provide abundant, nutritious food for man and increase the cattle and other living creatures. Hence performing yagna will itself becomes worship to the Lord. Hence, we must do these yagnas and rituals that benefit all. It will also bless the Nation.

'OngiyulakaLanda uttaman pErpADi' – The Lord, Narayana, took the form of Vamana for the benefit of the Devas. He has killed both brothers, Hiranyaksha and Hiranyakasipu. However, He could not do the same for emperor Bali. For one thing, Bali was the grandson of Lord's disciple, Prahallada. He has also performed many yajnas and yagas. He is very giving to the needy and always abides by the truth and follows dharma. Hence Potana says,

కలరున్ దాతలు, నిత్తురున్ ధన
ములన్, గామ్యార్థముల్ గొంచు వి
పులు నేతెంతురు, గాని, యావిని
బలిన్ బోలన్ వదాన్యుండు లే
డలఘుండై యొనరించె నధ్వర
శతం బా భార్గవానుజ్జచే
బలివేడన్ టడయంగ వచ్చు టపు
సంపల్లాభముల్ వామనా|| (Potana Bhavatatam)

Thus, Bali, who has earned name and fame among noble Brahmins, how can the Lord punish him as did with other Rakshasas? Hence, Lord personally went to Bali to beg a land from him.

Indeed, it is very degrading to go and beg somebody. Because of this, the infinite Lord has become a short young boy, Vamana, for begging from Bali. He asked for only three feet of land from the King. Once the King committed himself, knowing very well that he would never go back on his promise, the young boy started growing big, occupying the entire universe with his two steps. Potana describes his ever-expanding form with simple Telugu words – ఇంత *and* అంత *(this much and that much) with some visual projection of how the little boy started growing and occupying the entire cosmos.*

"ఇంతింతై వటు(డింతయె మటియు(
దా నింతై నభోవీథిపై
నంతై తోయదమండలాగ్రమున
కల్లంతై, ప్రభారాశిపై నంతై
చంద్రుని కంతయె ధ్రువుని పై
నంతై, మహర్వాటిపై నంతై
సత్యపదోన్న తుండగుచు
బ్రహ్మండాంత సంవర్ధియె." (Potana Bagavatam)

To that Lord who provides the shelter of all those who surrender to Him, Goda Devi says, 'shaatri neeraaDanaal' we are committing ourselves to undertake this ritual and gathering all those who are interested in this. To start this ritual, first, we are going to purify ourselves. By performing this ritual, Goda Devi says, 'theenginri naaDellaam thingal mummaari peydhu' the people will be blessed with good health without diseases and be free from famine and with needed rains every month, resulting in abundant crops, etc.

'Ongu perum senn nel oodu kayalugalap' with healthy crops growing abundantly, bending down all the way due to loaded heavy grains on its branches almost touching the water at the roots, with lively fishes running hither and thither – thus Goda Devi picturizes the prosperity that accompanies by performing a such sacred ritual. It means that in that Repalle, when abundant crops are blessing the residents, they being pious, do not harm these lovely fishes and leave them alive in the ponds without catching them for their consumption.

'poonguvalaip podhil pori vandu kan paduppath', the bees that are intoxicated by drinking the abundant honey from the fully blossomed flowers in the ponds, 'thaengaadhae pukkirundhu seerththa mulai patrivaanga', the big cows, after eating to the fullest extent, remained quietly without much movement after they entered their shelters, without disturbing anyone by moving their horns here and there and standing quietly with utmost satisfaction,

'kudam niraikkum vallal perum pasukkal neengaadha selvam' with abundant wealth and prosperity measured in terms of vessels full of milk and produce – thus, Goda Devi picturizes the prosperity that comes from performing these rituals. Thus, she glorifies the benefits we can get if we do these with utmost care and devotion.

The *'trivikramaavatara'* (Lord Vishnu when he takes the form occupying three words) by the touch of his feet, He purified the whole creation. Bali initially thought he was a great emperor and was well recognized for his generosity in giving a lot to deserving people. He felt small when this young bachelor boy asked meager three feet of land, that too measured by his tiny feet. Picturizing Bali's state of mind when the boy asks for only three feet of land, Potana says,

వసుధాఖండము వే(డితో, గజ
ముల౯ వాంఛించితో, వాజుల౯
వెస నూహించితో కోరితో యువ
తుల౯ వీక్షించి కాక్షించితో
పసిబాలుండవు నేర వీ వడుగ
నీ భాగ్యంటు లీపాటిగా
కసురేంద్రుండు పదత్రయంబడుగ
నీ యల్పంటు నీ నేర్చునే?

Thus, he was proud of his generosity. He felt insulted when the boy asked for only three feet of land instead of part of his empire, or lots of elephants, or many beautiful young girls to serve him – he could have any of these – but meager three tiny feet of land!

For one who thinks so highly of himself and is proud of his charities, it is imperative that he needs to be purified of his false values. His pride needs to be removed by a proper course of action for him to recognize his smallness in relation to the vastness of space and time. One who is proud of his wealth can lose his pride only when he loses all his wealth. Hence Lord Hari (one who steals!) not only removed the whole of his empire that he was so proud of but also made him humble and sattvic.

Sriihari replied to Brahma when he asked why you need to punish Bali, your devotee like this.

ఎవ్వని కరుణింప నిచ్చింతిని వాని
	యఖిల విత్తంటునేనపహరింతు
సంసారగురుమద స్తబ్దుడై(యెవ్వడు
	దెగడి లోకము నన్ను ధిక్కరించు
నత(డెల్ల కాలంటు నఖిల యోనులయందు
	బుట్టును దుర్గతి బొందు బిదప
విత్తవయో రూప విద్యా బలైశ్వర్య
	కర్మ జన్మంటుల గర్వముడిగి
యేకవిధమున విమలు(డై యెవ్వ(డుండు
వా(డు నాగూర్చి రక్షింపవలయువా(డు
స్తంభలోభాభిమాన సంసార విభవ
మత్తు(డై చెడనొల్ల(డు మత్సరుండు (Potana)

Lord responded that to those devotees who have surrendered, He will bless them by taking every worldly possession they have, which only acts as a distraction in their pursuit. Those who ignore Me due to their arrogance and long for only worldly possessions, they will be born again and again and suffer life after life even deprived of those worldly possessions.

Prahalada, the great devotee of the Lord, seeing his grandson, Bali, who became insignificant now after Hari removed his entire empire with his two feet, praises the Lord

ఇతనికి మున్ను నీ వింద్ర పదంబిచ్చి
    నేడు త్రిప్పుటయును నెఱియ మేలు
మోహనాహంకృతి మూలంటు గర్వాంధ
    తమస వికారంటు దాని మాన్పి
కరుణ రక్షించుటగాక, బంధించుటే?
    తత్త్వజ్ఞనకు మహేంద్రత్వ మేల?
నీ పాదకములంటు నియతి(గొల్చిన దాని(
    టోలునే సురరాజ భోగపరత?

గర్వమేపార(గన్నులు(గానరావు
చెవులు వినరావు చిత్తంటు సిక్కువడును
మఱిచు నీసేవలన్నియు మహిమ మాన్పి
మేలు సేసితి నీమేటిమెర సూపి|| - (Potana)
సావర్ణిమనువు వేళను, దేవేంద్రుండగు నితండు దేవతలకు దు
ర్బావిత మగునాచోటికి, రావించెద నంతమీ(ద రక్షింతు
దయన్. (Potana)

Thus, Prahalad says that it was only to bless his grandson Bali that Hari, who originally blessed him with the position of Indra, now removed everything from him to make him humble, thereby annihilating his ahankara (ego) and mamakara (being proud of his possessions). It is only to protect Bali, Hari did all this – thus praises Lord Narayana for His generosity showered on his grandson.

People pray to other Gods who can be easily reached to be blessed with wealth and material prosperity. In the process, they distance themselves from the real source of happiness. They try to increase their POT (possessions, obligations, and transactions) as though that is the very purpose of life itself. On the other hand, those who worship Hari, who steals everything, lose all their self-centered desires for external entities. They develop desires to reach the highest to secure divine blessings. They become dearer to the Lord. Just as Lord Hari, in the end, blessed Bali by becoming his gateman (filtering what can enter his mind and what should not). Hence Krishna says, those who have surrendered to Him completely, He takes care of their yoga and kshema, योगक्षेमम् वहाम्यहम्.

In addition, for those who have completely surrendered to Him, He also said, 'अहम् त्वाम् सर्व पापेभ्यो मोक्षयिष्यामि' – I will relieve you from all your sins and give you the liberation that you are longing for' – Hence Goda Devi says, 'Theenginri naadellaam', Lord has promised us that all our actions that are obstacles to our liberation will be destroyed. She further says, 'mum maari peydhu', Lord, in the end, provides us uncomparable, unlimited, and unending (the three un's) happiness we are longing for. Goda Devi says, perum senn nel Ongu, by surrendering to the Lord, one automatically enhances his satvic gunas, such as peace, forgiveness, large-heartedness, etc.

Moreover, by saying, 'Poonguvalaip podhil pori vandu kan paduppath', not only the good qualities will enhance, but the bad qualities that involve kaama, krodha, etc., the six fundamental enemies that disturb the peace of mind of an earnest seeker will get eliminated. In addition, by *'Neengaadha Selvam kudam niraikkum'*, she implies that one gets unbroken blessings of the Supreme Lord and, as a result, eternal happiness by His grace.

Hence, Goda Devi calls all the ladies, saying, 'You All Ladies! Those who are all interested in the highest goals in life, please join us in performing this sacred ritual'.

Pasuram:

మెలమెల్ల మినుమించి, మెయివెంచి
    లోకాల గొలిచిన పెరుమాళ్ళ(, గొలిచి మేము
నోమదానము సేయ తాములెల్లను డిందు
    నెల మూ(డువానలు నెమ్మి గురియు,
వెన్నువంగిన మళ్ళ(జెన్నొంందు కలువ పూ
    పొదలతో మించు తుమ్మెదలు మొదలు
కయ్యల నీటిలో(గాడలు కదలంగ
    దుడుకు టేడిసలు దుందుదుకు సేయు
కుండవొదుగుల పశువులు గోష్ఠములను
పిడికిలికి వెక్కసంటగు కొడుల(ట్టి
పిండ(గురియును కడవలు నిండ(బాలు
సంపదలు వెల్లవలు గట్టి పెంపుదనర.

PASURAM 4

Introduction:

In the ritual that will be performed during Margasira month (middle of December to the middle of January), Goda Devi is requesting the clouds in the sky to shower the plenty of water needed for the formers of Repalle.

ஆழிமழைக் கண்ணா! ஒன்று நீ கைகரவேல்
    ஆழியுள் புக்கு முகந்து கொடார்த்தேரி
ஊழி முதல்வன் உருவம் போல் மெய் கறுத்துப்
    பாழியந் தோளுடைப் பத்மநாபன் கையில்
ஆழிபோல் மின்னி, வலம்புரிபோல் நின்று அதிர்ந்து
    தாழாதே சார்ங்க முதைத்த சரமழை போல்
வாழ உலகினில் பெய்திடாய் நாங்களும்
    மார்கழி நீராட மகிழ்ந்து ஏல் ஓர் எம்பாவாய்.

Aazhi mazhaik kannaa onru nee kai karavael

Aazhi ul pukku mugandhu kodu aarthu aeri

Oozhi mudhalvan uruvam pol mey karuththup

Paazhiyam tholudaiya parpanaaban kaiyil

Aazhi pol minni valamburi pol ninru adhirndhu

Thaazhaadhae saarngam udhaiththa saramazhai pol

Vaazha ulaginil peydhidaay naangalum

Maargazhi neeraada magizhndhaelor embaavaay (4)

Goda Devi addresses the Rain God, '*Aazhi mazhaik kannaa*'- Oh! Parjanyaa! With a prayer. Without rain, there cannot be crops. Because of that, there will not be food for all living beings. पर्जन्यात् अन्न संभवः says Geeta. Just as Lord Sriman Narayana has taken the duty of protecting all lokas, God Parjanya took the responsibility to provide food for all beings. In the kathopanishat, it is said that all phenomenal forces (Gods with different portfolios) are bound to follow their assigned duties (laws governing them) under the control of the Supreme Lord. The physical laws governing the universe are fixed and ordained by the force that created them.

भयादस्याग्निस्तपति भयात्तपति सूर्यः
भयादिन्द्रश्च वायुश्च मृत्युर्धावति पश्चमः|
(Kathopanishat 2:6.3)

Addressing the God Parjanya, Goda Devi says, '*onru nee kai karavael*', please do not be greedy with us. Rain down freely all the water we need. The Rain God should not think that 'I have given rains before, but they have not yet prayed for me to rain here now. He needs to do what is required, following the rules. पर्जन्यवलक्षण्प्रवृत्तिः is vyakarana rules. Hence, Goda Devi says, even though it is your nature to rain down as per rules, even if someone prays for it or not, we are asking you to give us plenty of water that we need since we depend on it.

How does the Rain God have water to pour down at different places, Goda Devi says, '*aazhi ul pukku mugandhu kodu aarthu aeri'* , please go and enter the ocean, and drink water to your fullest capacity and quickly raise above the ocean and come back to the lands. The Oceans have unlimited water stored in them. Yet not a drop of that water is drinkable as the saying goes, 'water, water everywhere, not a drop to drink'. It is like misers having a lot of money, but what is the use? They will not give to anybody, nor will they enjoy themselves.

> "ఆస్తికు(డెని, విత్తము సమస్తము
> పాత్రల హస్తసాత్కృతే
> శస్తము, వెచ్చటెట్టుట ప్రశస్తము
> భోగరసానుభూతికై,
> నాస్తికు(డెని, (దానుదిన కర్థుల
> కియ్యక దాచిపెట్టు చా
> దస్తపు చేతకున్ కతమతర్క్యము
> సుంత, అగమ్య మెంతయున్" (My Shantivilasamu)

What happens to the wealth that the misers have saved so much wealth that they neither enjoyed nor shared with anyone else? From those misers, either the Government, noble people, or robbers, by threatening or stealing or using other means to rob away their wealth and use it. If instead, the money is donated for some right causes, then both the receivers and the donors will also benefit.

Even though the sea water is salty and undrinkable, clouds taking away that water and purifying it make it drinkable.

स्न्तप्रायसि संस्थितस्ययसोनामापि न श्रूयते
मुक्ताकारतया तदेव नलेनी पत्रस्थितम् द्रस्यते
अंतस्सागर शुक्ति मध्यपतितम् तन्मौक्तिकम् जातते
प्राणाधम मध्यमोत्तम जुषामेवंविधा वृत्तयः||
(Bhartruhari)

"నీరము తప్త లోహమున నిల్చి
    యనామకమై నశించు నా
నీరమె ముత్యమట్లు నళినీదళ
    సంస్థితమై తనర్చు, నా
నీరమె శుక్తిలో(బడి మణిత్వము(
    గాంచు సమంచితప్రభన్
బొరుష వృత్తులిట్లధము మధ్యము
    నుత్తము(గొల్చువారికిన్ " (Telugu-Yenugu
Lakshmana kavi)

The water drops that fall in a copper vessel will slowly get lost without a trace. If it falls on the lotus leaf, the water drop will shine like a pearl, and the same water if it falls 'sukti – 'will turn itself into a pearl. Thus, depending on where it lands, an object's value changes. By eating some useless grass, the cow is giving back tasty milk. Drinking that milk, a snake becomes a source of poison.

In the same way, Oh! Parjanya! Drink that useless salty water from the ocean. You are part of the universal protector, Lord Narayana. Lord uses you to get His work done. Nothing can affect Him. The poisonous milk of the demon Putana did not cause any harm to little Krishna. It got digested without a problem. In the same way, you being part of Him, nothing happens when you drink the useless waters of the Ocean to your fullest extent. By converting it into good water that everyone can drink, you get doubly blessed by the Lord for doing His assigned job.

For the true devotees, everything appears as the His manifestation and glory. Goda Divi sees the clouds as the form of Lord Vishnu and describes them as *'oozhi mudhalvan uruvam pol mey karu'*, the form of the dark color of the Shreeman Narayana's body.

Lord is the very source of the creation. *'oozhi mudhalvan'*. जन्माद्यस्य यतः is the definition for Iswara by Brahmasutras and Upanishads – that is the very source, sustenance, and dissolution for the creation, 'यतोवा इमानि भूतानि जायंते, येन जातानि जीवंति, यत्पयम् त्यभिसम् वशंतीति' says Tai. Up., that is Brahman or Paramaatma. Mundaka Up. says,

यत्तदद्रेश्य मग्राह्य मवर्णम्, अचक्षु श्रोत्रम्, तदपाणि पादम्
नित्यम् विभुम् सर्वगतम् सुसूक्ष्मम्
तत् अव्ययम् तद्भूत योनिम्, परिपश्यंति धीराः|

He is ungraspable by the five senses, who does not have body parts made of Prakriti, is yet very source for all beings and the world, and is also the material cause for the universe. He is none other than Shreeman Narayana only.

Hence Mahopanishat says:

अथ पुरुषो ह वै नारायणो2 कामयतः प्रजासृजेयेति।
नारायणात्प्राणो जायते।
मन स्सर्वेंद्रियाणि च, खम् वायुज्र्योतिरापः पृथिवी
विश्वस्य धारिणी
नारायणा द्ब्रह्मा जायते, नारायणाद्रुद्रो जायते।
(Mahopanishat)

అంత పురుషోత్తముడు నారాయణుండు
స్వాంతమ్ములో(దలచె(ట్రజస్పృష్టి సేయ
ట్రాణమ్ము గలిగె నారాయణుని నుండి
హృదయాది కిరణ సముదయమ్ము గలిగె
ఆకసమ్మును గలిగె నగ్ని యప్పులును
అఖిలమున కాధారమైన ధారణియు
జనియించె నారాయణుని నుండి ట్రహ్మ
జనియించె నారాయణుని నుండి శివుడు... (my
Naarayaneeyam)

Thus, Upanishads declare that the entire universe consists of fourteen lokas, and all the movable and immovable living beings are created from Shreeman Narayana only.

Poets describe Him as possessing blue color. Goda Devi uses this analogy to address the clouds as part of Narayana.

'paazhiyam tholudaiya parpanaaban kaiyil aazhi pol minni', Lord Narayana is also called Lord Padmanabha

(one with a lotus-like belly button) is also said to have long and beautiful shoulders and hands. सुभुजो दुर्धरो वाग्मी – says Vishnusaharanaamavali – He has such a belly button from which lotus came out it and from that lotus, the creator of the worlds, Brahmaji, was born.

चकासतम् ज्याकिणकर्कशै शशुभै
श्चतुर्भिराजानु विलंबिभिर्भुजै:
प्रियावतम् सोत्पल कर्णभूषण
श्लथालकाबंधविमर्दशंसिसिभि: (sthotraratnam)

After having kept as a pillow for Goddes Lakshmi, the Lord's hands have acquired the enchanting shining of earrings and the other head jewelry and the glory of her well-groomed long, beautiful hair, and in the right hand that contained Sudarshana chakram or disk with thousand spikes shining brilliantly by reflecting light. Oh! Could! You too, show your brilliant flashes of lightning reciprocating the Lord's glory.

"valamburi pol ninru adhirndhu" – On the Lord's left hand, there is *'Panchajanyam'* conch reflecting the essence of thundering knowledge while frightening enemies. In the same way, you make a thundering noise that can frighten all the enemies that perturb the tranquil atmosphere.

It is not sufficient just to have flashes of lightning and thunder.

'thaazhaadhae saarngam udhaiththa saramazhai pol vaazha ulaginil peydhidaay'

Just as Shreeman Narayana is ready to come immediately without waiting even for a second, to protect His devotees and ready to punish those that perform evil deeds for their selfish ends, and ready to shower with the required protective weapons, you too shower rains like enemies, the famine, etc. will not come in to disturb the prosperity of the people. Like friends, the corps and the produce will arise. In that way, we too, *'maargazhi neeraada magizhndhaelor'* enjoy the Margari month's rituals and the taking bath in the sacred pushkarini waters', says Goda Devi.

Thus, this ritual not only benefits society but also pleases the Lord of the universe. We are only obliged to do actions that benefit the society at large and also those that will be pleasing to the Lord. Our actions not only benefit us but also will be helpful to society. All the earnings we need to use for the benefit of society only. The earned wealth is not to be used for self-aggrandizement but to be used for society at large. This is the essence of the message Goda Devi is giving us.

Pasuram:

కుంచించుకొన(టోకు కొంచమేనియు దాన

హస్తమో యన్న, వర్షాధినాథ,

కడలి లోనికి(జొచ్చి కడుపార నీరాని

త్రె(చి, నింగికి నెక్కి రే(గి సా(గి,

జగదాదికారణ శ్యామలవిగ్రహ

పద్మనాభుని దీర్ఘబాహుయుగళి

¹సరియట్లు మెరపుల(బరపుచు, ²వలముरి

కైవడి గంభీర గర్భ లెస(గ

పైరు పచ్చల జగతి సంపదలు పొదల

³నాగ్రహోయణి మేము నీరాడి మురియ

శార్ఙ కార్ముక నిర్గత శరవిధాన

వాన(గురియుము వేగ ననూనదాన||

----

¹చక్రము, ²శంఖము, ³మార్గశిరము.

PASURAM 5

Introduction:

For gaining moksha or liberation from the cycle of birth and death, karma is not the path as it will only reinforce binding to the Prakriti. It is said that Karmas are responsible for our birth and death cycles. Hence it is essential to remove them entirely for spiritual evolution, which is not easy. Hence Goda Devi says the easiest path involves worship of the Lord, His service, singing His glories, etc., to help eliminate all the Karmas that are a hindrance to liberation.

Pasuram:

மாயனை மன்னு வடமதுரை மைந்தனைத்
    தூய பெருநீர் யமுனைத் துறைவனை
ஆயர் குலத்தினில் தோன்றும் அணி விளக்கைத்
    தாயைக் குடல் விளக்கஞ் செய்த தாமோதரனை
தூயோமாய் வந்து நாம் தூமலர் தூவித் தொழுது
    வாயினால் பாடி மனத்தினால் சிந்திக்க
போய பிழையும் புகுதருவான் நின்றனவும்
    தீயினில் தூசாகும் செப்பு ஏல் ஓர் எம்பாவாய்.

Maayanai mannu vada madhurai maindhanaith

Thooya peru neer yamunaith thuraivanai

Aayar kulaththinil thonrum ani vilakkaith

Thaayaik kudal vilakkam seydha dhaamodharanaith

Thooyomaay vandhu naam thoomalar thoovith thozhudhu

Vaayinaal paadi manaththinaal sindhikkap

Poya pizhaiyum pugudharuvaan ninranavum

Theeyinil thoosaagum cheppaelor embaavaay (5)

Meaning: By worshiping with the pure mind and devotional (mind that is offering than begging for more sense objects) the Lord who is the master of Maaya, but born in Mathura, running around happily in the banks of Yamuna as little Shree Krishna, all our sanchita and aagaami karmas will get burned away like the huge cotton mountain getting burned with a small spark of fire.

अजोपि सन्नव्ययात्मा भूतानामीश्वरोSपि सन्।
प्रकृतिम् स्वामधिष्टाय संभवाम्यात्ममायया॥
(Geeta 4:6)

Shreeman Narayana, Lord of all beings, even though He is beyond the cycle of birth and death, takes the suitable body required to solve an otherwise unsolvable problem by His will.

यदा यदा हि धर्मस्य ग्लानिर्भवति भारत।
अभ्युत्थान मधर्मस्य तदात्मनम् सृजाम्याहम्।
(Geeta 4:7)

Thus, He says, He is born to uplift dharma whenever and wherever strong adverse elements arise to destroy the dharma. One who is more brilliant than thousands of suns, recognizing that humans cannot experience such brilliance, He covers it up and takes birth in the needed forms by using His power of Maaya.

The people who lived on the northern side of Mathura were luckier than those who lived on the southern side of Mathura, as they could witness the glorious acts of Lord Krishna. They could experience His ruling directly. By becoming the Leader of that Mathura.

Goda Devi says, *'thooya peru neer yamunaith thuraivanai'*, Yamuna River got blessed and purified by first touching the feet of the Lord in the form of baby Krishna, and then giving a way to facilitate Vasudeva to carry Him to Gokula to Nanda's place, facilitating for Gopies to play around with Krishna on its shores. Through these plays, Yamana and its shores near Gokula became doubly blessed. Such is the Glory of the Lord.

'aayar kulaththinil thonrum', even though born in a royal family, choose to become a cowherd and blessed the Gokula people.

ఏమి నోము ఫలమొ యింత ప్రొద్దెక వార్త
వింటి మటలలార వీను లలర
మన యశోద చిన్ని మగవాని(గనెన(ట
చూచి వత్త మమ్మ! సుదతులార!| (Potana)

Little Krishna born as a baby in their house, was itself a great blessing for the couple Nanda and Yasoda, and what to talk about little Krishna playfully growing up as a baby, with his mischievous activities; it must be due to many merits that they have earned in their past lives.

If one thinks logically, it is not convincing that the Lord of the entire universe has to take birth in this world of prakruti, just to punish some wicked ones who are violating the Dharma.

జగముల(బ్రోచు బాధ్యత
    భుజావళి(దాలిచి నీవు సాధులన్
సుదతుల బాధ పెట్టు, వర సుందరులన్
    బలవంతపెట్టు, దుండ
గులను రూపుమాపుటకు,
    నై గమధర్మము లింపు పెంపునేం
దగ, విభవావతారు(డయినావట
    మాధవ చెన్నకేశవా||

కాని నా కది నచ్చలేదు విను,
    సంకల్ప్వైక సంసిద్ధకా-
మా నీ యిచ్చ యొకండె రక్షి
    గమిన్ మాయింప దక్షంటు గా
దా? నీ శార్ఙ్గము లేద? చక్రమును
    లేదా? పంప(బోదా? అరిం
దాసై దా విదళించ వచ్చునుగదా
    దామోదరా? కేశవా?

గోటను బోవుదానికయి గొడ్డలి
    దెచ్చిన భంగి నీవు నీ
పెటను కోటన్ విడిచి

పెండ్లము పానుపు వెంటరా(గ నీ
రాట నిశాట జాల్మ నివహంటు
నడంపగ వచ్చితన్న, నా
మాటను విన్న, నవ్వరె?
రమారమణీధవ చెన్న కేశవా. (My Keshava prappatti)

To stop the dagger thrown by Durvaasa towards
Amabarisha did you come down yourself from Vaikuntam?
Didn't you send your chakram/disk Sudarshana to do
that job? Not only the chakram destroyed the dagger but
chased the Durvasa all over the universe until he fell at the
feet of Ambarisha to spare his life. Did it not do all that
just by your will?

భువి దూఅిన్ భువి దూఙు, నభ్ది(జొ ర
నభ్దిన్ జొచ్చు నుద్వేగియై
దివి(ట్రొకన్ దివి(ట్రొకు, దిక్కులకు(
టొ దిగ్వ్వధులన్ టొవు(జి
క్క వెసన్ గ్రుంగిన(గ్రుంగు, నిల్వ
నిలుచున్ గ్రేడింప(గ్రేడించు నో
క్కవడిన్ దాపసు వెంటనంటి
హరిచక్రం టన్యదుర్వ్యక్రమై.

ఏ లోకంటున కైన వెంట(టడి తో
నేతెంచు చక్రానల
జ్వాలల్ మానుపువారు లేమి(
జని దేవజ్యేష్ఠు లోకేశు వా(
డాలోకించి, "విధాత విశ్వ
జననవ్యాపార పారిణ రే

ఖలీలేక్షణ చూడవే కరుణ(
    జక్రంటున్ నివారింపవే". (Potana)

Potana describes: The Rishi Durvasa went to all three lokas and sought the help of the Lords, Shiva, Brahma, and Vishnu but could not get any help in stopping the 'chakram' that was chasing him all the time, and at last came back to Ambarish, on whom he initially sent a sword to kill, requesting to pardon him and save him from the Vishnu-chakram. It is all due to the wish of the Lord, who makes sure no one insults his devotees. By His mere wish, He could accomplish the work; why does He have to come down to earth to take birth just to disciple some bad Rakshasas? By His mere will, they could have got destroyed.

Just to kill a crocodile that caught Gajendra or to punish Sishupala, who exceeded his allowed hundred cases of abuse, He does not have to come down from His Vaikunta. He could have just commanded His chakra to do the job.

Hence, it is not just to punish the wicked He comes down to earth. He comes down Himself because,

తావక మంజుముగ్ధ శిశుతన్
    గన(గోరిన భక్త కోటికిన్
నీ వదనేందు బింట రమణీయత
    గోరిన గోపికాళికిన్
స్వావనదక్షు సేవ సలుపంగ(
    దలచిన యార్త కోటికిన్

నీవు ముదంటు(గూర్ప(గ జనించితి
వంచు(దలంతు కేశవా. (My Keshava pravakti)

Many devotees who wanted to see your enchanting beauty, your playful activities, desiring to offer themselves to you as Gopies did, or to serve you in any capacity that they can – only to fulfill their wishes, you are born again and again in different forms – this is what I think.

Thus, to fulfill such desires only, Goda Devi says, *'thaayaik kudal vilakkam seydha'* you first blessed Devaki Devi's womb and later grew up doing all the baby pranks with Yasoda Devi.

Once, at the end of Svaayambhuva manu regime, the noblest couple, Vrushni and Prajapati named Sutapundu did many, many years of tapas (penance). You appeared to them ready to fulfill whatever desires they had. Since their delusion is not completely gone, instead of asking for Moksha, they said they would be very happy if the Lord was born to them as a baby to take care of Him. Very pleased by their desire, you are born to them three times as a baby.

అదితియు కశ్యపు(డన(గా
విదితులరగు మీకు(గుఱుచవేషంటున నే
నుదయించితి వామను(డన
ద్రిదశేంద్రానుజు(డనై ద్వితీయ భవమునన.

ఇప్పుడు మూ(డవ బామున(
దప్పక మీ కిరువురకును తనయు(డ నైతిన

చెప్పితి పూర్వము మీయం
దెప్పటికిని లేదు జన్మమిటపై నాకున్| (Potana)

In the same way, during the time of Rama, 'पुंसां मोहनरूपाय' many, including munis, felt like embracing the Lord but could not do so since Rama was a man. Hence Lord blessed them by being born in a beautiful form as Lord Krishna, while the Munis were born as Gopikas in Repalle so that they could now play and embrace the Lord of their desire.

If the Lord solves the problem of getting rid of the bad people by sending his chakram while staying in Vaikunata, how can He fulfill the desires of his devotees? Hence, He is willing to be born among the people blessing the wombs of his mothers while participating in His divine play.

While He holds the whole universe in his stomach (Damodara), yet out of love for His mother, Yasoda, He let Himself be bound by her rope. The one that is carrying many universes inside, that stomach, how can it be tied by small rope using which Yosoda Devi is trying to tie Him. Hence Potana says,

చిక్క(డు సిరికా(గిటిలో(
జిక్క(డు సనకాది యోగిచిత్తాబ్జములన్
జిక్క(డు శ్రుతిలతికావళి(
జిక్కె నత(డు లీల(దల్లిచేతన్ తోలన్|

తజ్జనని లో(గిటం గల
రజ్జుపరంపరల గ్రమ్మఖిన్ సుతు(గట్టన్

బొజ్జ దిరిగి రాదయ్యె జ
గజ్జాలము లున్న బొజ్జ(గట్టన వశమే?

బంధవిమోచకు(డీశు(డు
బంధింపన్ తెన(గు జనని పాటోర్చి సుహృత
బంధు(డు గావున, జననీ
బంధంబున(గట్టువడియె పాటించి నృపా| ((Potana)

The one who does not want to get bound by the embrace of Goddess Laksmi, the one who does not want to get caught by the grate sages like Sanaka, etc. in their minds, yet got bound by the innocent cowherd lady, Yasoda Devi – what a divine play is this! Even when Yasoda Devi tried to bind him with a rope but found that however big the rope was, it became shorter by a few inches until, while wondering how to solve the problem, out of compassion for his mother, he let himself bound by the rope. He is the one who removes all bindings for people, yet He let himself bound by her; what a wonder!

That is the nature of Lord Damadara. To that Lord, Goda Devi says: *'thooyomaay vandhu naam thoomalar thoovith thozhudhu Vaayinaal paadi manaththinaal sindhikkap'*

Once we have purified our bodies by taking a bath in the river, and by singing the glories of Lord Hari, and keeping the mind single-pointed prayer to the Lord, doing His prayers using sacred flowers and thus purifying mentally, speech-wise, and duties-wise, then for us, *'poya pizhaiyum pugudharuvaan ninranavum theeyinil thoosaagum'*, all our sanchita and aagaami karmas will get burned away like the cotton ball by a spec of fire.

Karmas are divided into three types sanchita, aagaami and praarabhda. The total karma account stored is called Sanchita karma; the results of the actions that come in the future are called aagaami, and the actions or karmas we brought with us to exhaust in this life are called praarabhda. All three karmas form obstacles for our moksha. Krishna says, ममैवांशो जीवलोके जीवभूतस्सनातनः (Geeta 15:7). Even though all Jeevas are part of my chit and ananda swaruupam, they get fascinated by my Prakruti and get trapped by forgetting their true nature and thus get separated from Me. They get more and more trapped in this samsara by indulging in sense pleasures and continuously going after them, life after life.

आत्मानम् रथिनम् विद्धि शरीरम् रथमेव तु
बुद्धिम् तु सारथिम् विद्धि मनः प्रग्रहमेव च।

इंद्रियाणि हयानाहुः विषयां स्तेषु गोचरान्।
आत्मेंद्रिय मनोयुक्तम् भोक्तेत्याहुर्मनीषिणः॥

यस्त्वविज्ञानवान् भवति युक्तेन मनसा सदा।
तस्येन्द्रियाणि वश्यानि सदश्चा इव सारथेः॥

यस्त्वविज्ञानवान् भवति अमनस्कः सदाऽशुचिः
न स तत्पदमाप्नोति संसारम् चाधिगच्छति।
यस्तु विज्ञानवान्भवति समनस्कः सदा शुचिः
न तु तत्पदमाप्नोति यस्माद्भूयो न जायते।

विज्ञान सारथिर्यस्तु मनः प्रग्रहवान्नरः
सोऽध्वनः पारमाप्नोति तिद्विष्णोः परमम् पदम्|
(Kathopanishat 3.9 :3)

The body is like a chariot. The senses are like horses. Mind is like reins; Intellect is the driver. With good intellect and a sound mind ensuring that the senses do not go in the wrong direction, ensuring they go only in the right direction, without causing damage to the chariot and the driver, is the best approach. In that way, the self will reach the final goal. The Jeeva will attain the moksha that is ever permanent. On the other hand, with uncontrollable horses and the intellect and the mind taking the chariot in the wrong direction, the chariot and the driver will get hurt and sometimes get damaged beyond repair. Such persons with impure minds and intellect following the wrong paths will end up suffering more and more, life after life.

Hence in Manucharitra, Allasani Peddana provides, how Pravara, rejected Varudhini when she approached him offering herself for sense pleasures. Pravara who is devoted to higher values in life says:

తరుణీ ! రేపును మాపుహవ్యముల
చేతన దృష్పుడౌ వహ్ని స
త్కరుణాదృష్టి నొసంగు సౌఖ్యము
లెఱుంగన్ శక్యమే, నీకు, నా
కరణుల్ దర్భలు నగ్నులున్ ప్రియము
లై నట్లన్యముల్ గా వొడల్

తిరమే? చెప్పకు మిట్టి తుచ్ఛ
సుఖముల4 మీసాలపై(దేనియలో. (Peddana)

Rejected her proposal by saying the pleasures he gets by performing his daily rituals to the Lord using the daily homam provide the greatest happiness than the baser pleasure that she is offering.

Hence, one who is intelligent will not go after the temporary sense- pleasures, leaving the eternal happiness that one can get by devotion to the Lord. The sense-pleasures can give some immediate happiness but only lead to long-lasting suffering.

Even those who perform good actions with the expectation of lasting pleasures may go to heaven and enjoy more sense-pleasures there. Yet once the account is over, they will be pushed out of those places as Geeta says, क्षीणे पुण्ये मर्त्यलोकम् विशंति, after the exhaustion of their merits (punyam) they will be pushed back to earth to do more actions. One can go back and forth with an endless cycle unless one turns his attention toward the Lord with devotion, as the famous sloka below says.

पुनरपि जननम् पुनरपि मरणम्, पुनरपि जननीजठरे शयनम्|
इह संसारे बहु दुस्तारे कृपयाSपारे पाहि मुरारे|
(Bhajagovindam)

After many, many births, due to the accumulated merits, one gets exposed to the proper teacher who directs his mind towards the Lord, by whose grace he reaches the highest.

Thus, the karmas, both good and bad, are obstacles to further progress. Would it make any difference if one is bound by iron or golden shackles?

అన్నము వేలె హేతువగు నంట
   యహమ్ము(న బాము గొంటకై
పున్నెము గూడ, కర్మమును
   భోగములేక నశించి పోవునే?
అన్నెము పున్నెమున్ వలన నన్య
   యసౌఖ్య పదార్థళమ్ము, నే
నన్ని ఫలాశవీడి భవదర్పణ
   సేయ(గ(జూతు కేశవా| (My Keshava prapatti)

Hence one must burn away both good and bad karmas, and sanchita and aagaami karmas. That can only be done by completely surrendering oneself to the Lord Narayana.

పుట్టుకు విత్తు కర్మ మది
   పున్నెము నన్నెమునైన భుక్తికై
పుట్టువు నెత్తు జీవి యది
   పొల్లోనరించిన దగ్ధ కర్ము(డై
పుట్ట(డు మీ(ద, నందులకు బోధ
   మొనర్చెను సాంఖ్యయోగమున్
దొట్టియుపాయముల్ యదు
   సుతుండు ప్రపన్న మహేన్ద్రసూతికిన్ (My Yatiraajeeyam)

There are many ways how one can reduce their karmas.

భజ ముకుందుని భజ ముకుందుని
　　భజ ముకుందుని తమ్ముడా
చావుకాలము దాపురించిన
　　కావ పేవియు మూఢుడా? (My Translation of Bhajagovindam)

Hence, as Shankara says, there is only one to protect us, Lord Mukunda. Hence pray to the Lord – that is the best approach. Food, drinks, house, lands, wealth, bank accounts, wife and children, etc. will not protect us from this cycle of birth and death and karmas.

రక్షణ యన్న, మేనునకు రాం
　　కవముల్ నునుపట్టు పుట్టముల్
కుక్షికి(బాయసాన్నములు
　　కూరలు భక్ష్యములించు పాన కా
లక్షికి రమ్యవస్తువు లనామయమున్
　　ధనమున్ గృహమ్ములా?
మోక్షముగాక, చచ్చుచును(
　　టుట్టుచు(గుండెడి జీవకోటికిన్| (My Yatiraajeeyam)

Hence, only Mukunda can give us the moksha we all long for. Mukunda also means the one who gives moksha. That name is suitable for Him since He alone can give moksha. Hence Shankaracharya says to worship him in his Bhajagovindam sloka.

Goda Devi also says pray to Damodara with a pure mind, speech, and actions – manasaa, vaachaa, karmanaa.

Using the mind, meditate on him, using the tongue sing His glories, and with hands, worship Him with beautiful flowers. If we do that as she says, all our sanchita and aagaami karmas will get burned away completely like a giant cotton hill with a tiny spark from the fire.

Because of the praarabhda karma this current body, mind, etc., are maintained, which need to be used in the devotional activities of the Lord. Hence, Goda Devi calls all the Repalle girls to wake up and come and join her in the Margazi ritual.

Paasuram:

మాయలమారియై మధురలో జన్మించె
　　గొల్ల కొలమ్ముస(దల్లి కడుపు
విలసిల్ల(జేసి, మంగళ దీపమగుచు, కా
　　ళిందితీరాన కేళీవినోద
ముల సల్పే నట్టి దామోదరు మన మెల్ల
　　స్నాతలై పూతలై నతు లొనర్చి
కమ్మని పూవుల(గడక పాదారవిం
　　దమ్ము లర్పించి చిత్తమ్ముననందు
ధ్యానమొనరించి పాట నేరాడ పాడ,
న పునరావృత్తి పద గోపురార్గళములు
సంచితాగామి కర్మలు సమసిపోవు
కాలదే నిప్పులోబడ్డ తూలరాశి.

PASURAM 6

Introduction:

The next ten pasurams involve Goda Devi calling the Repalle girls to join her in the Margasirai ritual after purifying themselves by bathing in the river's fresh waters.

Periyalvar – tirupallandu sloka;

పెరుమాళ్ళ సేవలో మురిపమ్ము గలదేని
కుడిటడిగ నిలవుడీ నడికట్టు బిగగట్టి
కడుపు కూటికి పెతలబడు టడుగులను మేము
రానీము మాగుంపులోని కేరిని గూడ| (My Mangalaashaasanamu)

Pasuram 6:

புள்ளும் சிலம்பின காண் புள்ளரையன் கோயிலில்
    வெள்ளை விளிசங்கின் பேரரவம் கேட்டிலையோ?
பிள்ளாய் எழுந்திராய்! பேய்முலை நஞ்சுண்டு
    கள்ளச் சகடம் கலக் கழியக் காலோச்சி
வெள்ளத் தரவில் துயில் அமர்ந்த வித்தினை
    உள்ளத்துக் கொண்டு முனிவர்களும் யோகிகளும்
மெள்ள எழுந்து அரியென்ற பேரரவம்
    உள்ளம் புகுந்து குளிர்ந்து ஏல் ஓர் எம்பாவாய்

Pullum silambina kaan pullaraiyan koyilil

Vellai vili sangin paeraravam kaettilaiyo

Pillaay ezhundhiraay paey mulai nanchundu

Kallach chakatam kalakkazhiyak kaalochchi

Vellaththaravil thuyilamarndha viththinai

Ullaththuk kondu munivargalum yogigalum

Mella ezhundhu ari enra paeraravam

Ullam pugundhu kulirndhaelor embaavaay (6)

Oh! Young girl! You are still sleeping! The birds are awake and making noise. The conchs are being blown in the temple inviting all the devotees to come. The sages and the yogis got up in the very early morning (brahmamuhurtham) and recited loudly the Lord's thousands of names. Hearing Lord's glories makes us delightful. Why are you still sleeping when it is time for all of us to go and purify ourselves in preparation for the ritual?

Commentary: Smruti says, ब्राह्मी मुहूर्ते बुध्येत

The shrutis and smritis are intended for human beings and not for setting rules of living for the birds and animals. Nature controls them. For them, the intellect is not evolved to think, formulate, or follow the rules. For human beings, the case is different. Their intellect is evolved and can be developed through proper education. For that, rigid rules must be followed during the development stage. Hence, human beings can control their lives to some extent their nature and formulate the rules to follow for happy living. They can also live as they wish, following their destiny, and they will be accountable for their actions via agami karma. They can either go on the wrong path by indulging themselves with sense objects or control their senses and redirect their mind towards the Lord. The animals cannot do that as they cannot control their nature. When they are hungry, they eat whatever is available that is eatable, sleep when they are tired, and do excretion when nature demands. Since there is no will to act, they only exhaust their karma but do not accumulate new ones.

Prakruti, or Nature, follows the ordained rules of the Lord. For example, a clock on the wall works if it is supported by mechanical or electrical energy. It will not stop or start of its own will. Its utility depends on the owner, the human being. Nature makes the birds wake up early in the morning, make familiar noises, and move in the direction in search of food. Nature, using the birds, lets us know that it is time for us to get up too. Hence Goda Devi says, Oh! You intelligent Ladies! Birds, dictated by Nature, already got up and made noises informing us that it was time for us to get up! You have all committed to performing the Margali Maasam ritual, yet why are you still sleeping? It is high time for you to get up. Please get up; it is already getting late.

'*pullaraiyan koyilil vellai vili sangin paeraravam kaettilaiyo*', Oh! Lady! You may think these useless birds with no time concept get up whenever they want, and why should we care about them? Then listen. The temple priests have already come to the temple to do their daily worship of the Lord, who rides on the big bird, Garuda. They are now blowing their conches, inviting all the devotees to come to the temple for prayers. It is not feeble but loud for everyone in the village to hear. The sound of the conches is very special at the temple, reminding all of us it is time for our prayers. We hear those sounds every day in the temple of Lord Vishnu. Have you not heard those sounds today? *'pillaay'* – Oh! Lady! Even though you are grown up but still act like a small girl! It is not the age but acting responsibly as needed makes one mature. At least get up now!

'munivargalum yogigalum mella ezhundhu ari enra paeraravam' The sages and the yogis have already got up very early and are singing the glories of Lord Hari.

नामस्मरणा दन्योपायम् न हि पस्यामो भवतरणे।
राम हरे कृष्ण हरे तव नाम सदाऽनुवदामि हरे।
(Dashavatara stotrams)

Thus, a seeker says there is nothing more valuable than chanting the name of Lord Hari for his salvation.

A Jeeva who got caught up in this cycle of birth and death after evolving from insects to birds to animals and at last, due to the grace of the Lord, birth in the human form, prays for the Lord's blessings, as the poem below says.

కరుణాసింధువు నీవుగా, తృణ

ముగా కంజంటుగా మ్రానుగా
పురువుంగా విహగంటుగా మృగ
ముగా పుట్టించి గిట్టించినన్
వరుసన్ మర్త్యనిగా నొనర్చి మరి
నీ పాదారవిందద్వయీ
వరివస్యా సుకృతంటు గూర్చితివి
దేవా! మాధవా! కేశవా! (My Keshavaprapatti)

Thus, now we are brought up to the stage of the human form with intelligence to think about what is right and wrong. We are also blessed with Veda Shastras, following which we can evolve further with the grace of the Lord.

జీవుల మేలుకై వెడల(జేసితి
వాగమరాశి నీవు త
ద్భావము బోధసేయ(దగువారలు
జీవులె యంచు శాస్త్రముల్
నీవ రచింప(జేసితి ముని
ప్రవరావళిచేత(దాముగా
భావన సేయ(గా పలుభవం
టుల (బుట్టగ(జేసినాడవో
దేవ! తథాపి యీ ప్రజకు
తెల్వి జనింపమి నీదు దోసమా? (My Shantivilasam)

To perform the four purusharthas (dharma, artha, kaama, and moksha), the Lord has provided the needed Jnaanedriyas and karmendriyas for human beings. No other life form in this world is gifted with such complete equipment. Using his intellect, a human can bring into his control even a mighty elephant or ferocious tiger. That capacity is a blessing given to the human being by the Lord. Using these equipments properly, one has to turn his attention to self-evolution. For that, one needs to develop the mental capacity to control the sense organs from running to sense- enjoyments and in the process, becoming a slave to them. By controlling all the senses, a human being can turn toward the Lord for rapid evolution. Unfortunately, there are very few who are interested in evolving further. Most of the population, as we see, only seek sense-pleasures and thus get bound more and more to the cycle of birth and death.

కలదు పటిష్ఠ పాదయుగి
  కాపథమంది చరింప నెప్పుడున
కలదు రసజ్ఞ వాడియయి
  కారులు ప్రేలనె, దూఱులాడనే
కలదు మనీష యన్యగత
  కల్మషచర్చల నాచరింపనే
కలగియు నవ్వి , యాత్మహిత
  కర్మల కుంటిని మూ(గజంతువన| (My Shantivilasamu)

Lord has given this body the appropriate mind, intellect, and sense organs for rapid evolution to attain moksha. Human life becomes worthless if we do not use it for that purpose and only use it for selfish actions and sense-enjoyments. Shankaracharya says in Vivekachudamani 'मनुष्यत्वम् मुमुक्षुत्वम् महापुरुषसंश्रयम् दुर्लभम् त्रयमेवैतत् दैवानुग्रह हेतुकम्', being born as a human being, desire to seek liberation, and association with a proper teacher, all the three are very difficult to have. Only one gets them due to the blessings of the Lord.

Krishna says, 'मामेकम् शरणम् व्रज' (Geeta 18:66), surrender completely to Me alone. Now the ball is in your court, and you are free to choose. It is up to you. If you seek everlasting peace and liberation to attain moksha by surrendering to Me, I will promise to remove all the shackles that bind you to this Prakriti and liberate you from this samsara. That responsibility is mine.

Hence without any other dissipating thoughts, the sages and the yogis glorify the Lord with prayers and offerings from the moment they awake from sleep. To the root 'man' in Sanskrit, if we add 'in', it changes to 'u', from which the 'muni' sound forms. 'मन्यते इति मुनिः' means one who has jnaanam or knowledge of the supreme. Muni also means 'manana seelavan', one who contemplates the Lord's essence. One, who knows himself and knows about the essence of the universe, is a yogi – one who yoked his mind to the highest.

'योंतस्सुखोऽन्तरारामः तथांतर्जोतिरेवयः
स योगि ब्रह्मनिर्वाणम् ब्रह्मभूतो धिगच्छति।
(Geeta 5:24).

Yogi is the one who withdraws his mind from indulging outside on sense objects and turns his attention toward the supreme Lord.

Hence Goda Devi says – These munis and yogis are already got up and doing their prayers to the supreme Lord by singing His divine glories.

'*vellaththaravil thuyilamarndha, viththinai*', the supreme Lord is lying on the addisheha in the milky ocean in meditative sleep, but watching very closely if any mischievous people are trying to hurt His devotees anywhere in the universe. His sleep is not like ours, which is engulfed with tamas (we do not know even our own world and do not even know who we are when we are in a deep sleep state). For the Lord, who is in yoga nidra, His mind is spread all over His creation and fully aware of everything and every happening in the universe. Hence if a Jeeva anywhere in the corner of the universe cries saying, Hai! Krishna! 'पाहिमाम् यादव नंदना!' out of despair, like Gajendrea crying 'నీవే తప్ప నితఃపరంటెరుగ రక్షింపంగదే దీనునిన్' (Potana) saying that 'there is no one else other than you Oh! Lord! Please protect me! I am a desperate devotee of yours. Hearing that, Lord left everything and came running, leaving everything while the whole of His retinue followed Him behind. He did not tell even His believed Lakshmi, who is always there with Him. She ran behind Him to be in His service in case He needed her. Such is His commitment to save His devotees anywhere in this universe.

తన వెంచేయు పథంటు పేర్కొన
డనాథ స్త్రి జనాలాపముల్
వినెనో, ప్రుచ్చలు ప్రుచ్చిలించిరొ
ఖలుల్ వేదప్రపంచంటులన్

దనుజాధీశులు దేవతానగరిపై
దండెత్తిరో, సాధులన్
గని చక్రాయుధు(డేడి? చూపు(డని
ధిక్కరించిరో దుర్జనుల్| (Potana)

Gajendra was wondering why the Lord was delaying so much, imagining that He is busy protecting others. This is how Jeeva feels when he is desperate for help. However, the Lord waits until the Jeeva is ready to give up everything and completely surrender to Him. Only Lord Narayana was born as Lord Krishna to Devaki and Vasudeva to protect many devotees due to their many merits in their past life.

Lord Krishna is none other than Lord Narayana – as Vyasa Maharshi says,

"तमद्भुतम् बालकमंबुजेक्षणम्
चतुर्भुजम् शंखगदाद्युधायुधम्,
श्रीवत्सलक्ष्मम् गळशोभि कौस्तुभम्,
पीतांबरम् सांद्रपयोदसौभगम्,
महार्ह वैडूर्य किरीटकुंडल
त्विषा परिष्वक्त सहस्रकुंतलम्
उद्दाम कांच्यंगद कंकणादिभिः
विरोचमानम् वसुदेव ऐक्षत. (Bhagavatam)

Normally, Jeevas born because of their praarabda karma, from their mother's wombs. In contrast, Lord Krishna was born as a child with four hands with Panchajanya conch and the spinning disk (Sudarshana chakram), Gada (Koudaki mace), and sward (Nandaka) on the four hands, with the Lakshmi sign on his chest, Koustubam on his neck, golden ornaments around his hands, ears, with the crown on his head, to Devaki, as his father Vasudeva witnessed. Hence, he was called a divine child. He was a baalaka, i.e., a small boy. Since He is having Lakshmi mark on his chest, He is called Shree vatsudu. Shrevatsalakshmudu meaning on Sri, Goddes Lakshi, vatsala, having vaatsalyam (love). Lakshmi is also considered Prakriti, with its eightfold nature (ashta Lakshmi).

Lord Narayana is said to have two wives, Shreedevi and Bhuudevi. Purusha suuktam says, 'ह्रीश्चते लक्ष्मीश्च पत्न्यौ' - He is the husband of Lakshmi. Usually, when there are two wives, there will be jalousie between them. Bhudevi is the eldest wife. Yet Bhudevi treats her co-wife full of affection. Lakshmi Devi must have reciprocated it. The husband has two wives who love each other and their husband. Krishna represents such a husband. Krishna says:

परित्राणाय साधूनाम् विनाशाय च दुष्कृताम्‌|
धर्मसंस्थापनार्थाय संभवामि युगे युगे|| (Geeta 4:8)

Thus, Lord Narayana took birth as Lord Krishna to fulfill His promise. For creation and dissolution, He has kept Brahmaji and Shivaji in charge. He took the responsibility of maintaining the order in the Universe

Hence from the day, He was born as Krishna, He was on His mission, destroying the Rakshas that Kamsa had sent while providing shelter to the gopies and gopikas at

Repalle. First, *paey mulai nanchundu'*, He drank Putana's poisonous milk and, in the process, sucked her life out. For Him, Putana's poisonous milk or the gopikas butter must have tasted the same. He blessed Putana also.

किम् कालकूटः किमु वा यशोदा स्तन्यम् तव स्वादु वद प्रभो मे| (Tikkana)

Which one do you like more, is it Yasoda Devi's breast milk or Poison from Kalakuta? – Tikkana asked his Lord in the form of Hari Hara. However, this question also applies to Little Krishna, who drank Putana's poisonous milk and Yasoda Devi's sweet milk. Putana also took in her lap, little playful Krishna, and while fondling Him, started giving her poisonous milk. 'రక్కసి మగువ చిఱుతకొమరుని దిగిచి తొడల నడుమ నిడికొని, యొడలు నివురుచు, నెడనెడ మమతన్ గడలు కొలుపుచు' 'ఆకొన్న చిన్నియన్నచన్నుగుడువు" – అని చన్నిచ్చ సమయంటున, Potana's description of how Putana took little Krishna after fondling Him and then offering her breast for him to drink.

మెల్కొన్న తెఱ(గున మెల్లన కనువిచ్చి
క్రే(గంట(జూచుము(గిదికి నీళ్ళి
యావులించుచు జేతులాదరంటున(జూ(చి
యె(దిగిలియాకొన్న యోజ నూ(ది
బిగి చన్ను(గవ(గేల(బీడించి కబళించి
గ్రుక్క గ్రుక్కకు గుటుగుటుకు మనుచు
నీక రెండు గ్రుక్కల నువిద ప్రాణంబులు
సైతము మేనిలో సత్వ మెల్ల(.

ద్రావె! నదియును గుండెలు దల్లడిల్ల(
జిమ్మ(దిరుగుచు నిలువక శిరము వ్రాల,
నితర బాలుడ క్రియవా(డ వీవు గావు
చన్ను విడువుము విడువుము చాలు ననుచు.

నిబ్బరపు దప్పి మంటలు
ప్రబ్బిన ధ్రుతిలేక నేత్రపద హస్తంబుల్
గొబ్బున వివృతములుగ నా
గుబ్బగుచున్నట్టి కూ(త(గూలెన్ నేలన్| (Potana)

Thus, Little Krishna not only sucked her poisonous mill but also sucked her life out of that body.

पीत्वा विषाक्रममराधि कुरंगनेत्रा
स्तन्यम् सजीव पवमान ममारयद्यः
भक्तैस्समम् परमधाम निनाय ताम् तम्
गोपालबालकमुकुंद महम् नमामि| (My Mukundavilasamu)

The Lord sucked out not only poison but all her sins (*paapam*) too and gave her moksha – that is the generosity of the Lord when she came to offer something. In the same way, Goda Devi says, '*Kallach chakatam kalakkazhiyak kaalochchi*' the Lord broke all his attached bonds of Shatakasura and destroyed his body. Thus, singing many glories of the Lord, the Saints are waking us up.

Just as Devaki Devi got up slowly to ensure that it would not be painful as she was carrying in her womb the Lord of the entire universe, in the same way, '*viththinai ullaththhuk kondu*' the world as she carrying the Lord in its womb is slowly getting up.

अहम् कृत्स्नस्य जगतः प्रभवः प्रळयस्तथा
मत्तः परतरम् नान्यत्किंचि दस्ति धनंजय
मयि सर्व मिदम् प्रोतम् सूत्रे मणिगणा इव॥
(Geeta 6:6,7)

I am the root cause of everything in this creation. I am the very support of the whole universe; from Me, it arose, by Me, it is sustained, and into Me, it gets dissolved. Goda Devi says, thus, the glories of the Lord are being chanted in the Temple. Have you not heard, Oh! Young Lady! How come you are still sleeping?

'ullam pugundhu kulirndhaelor' – These prayers at the temple have entered our minds. Because of that, our minds have become very peaceful and serene.

For the one who is suffering from **the Sun's heat**, some shade and some cold drink will be very satisfying. But for those who do not get satisfied with these and the ones who are longing for mental peace, prayers to Lord only can give solace to their hearts.

'తాపత్రయాభీల దావాగ్నులాఱునే హరిమనీషామృత వృష్టిలేక' (Potana) the one who is suffering from the three fundamental sufferings cannot be at peace without the grace of God. It cannot be obtained without completely surrendering to Lord Hari. The three sufferings are a) Adhyaamika b) Adi Bhoutika, and c) Adi daivika. Adhyaamika involves the six fundamental enemies – kaama (selfish desires), krodha (anger), etc. Adi bhoutika involves the suffering caused by others, and Adi daivika involves external obstacles that are beyond our control – Extreme hot, extreme cold, too much rain, too little rain, etc. The suffering at the mental level can only be removed by turning the mind towards the Lord, chanting his name, singing His glories, listening to His stories, etc. Hence, the sages and the yogis spend all their time in these activities and thus keep their minds peaceful and serene. Oh! Lady! How can you hear these prayers when you have closed your doors and still sleeping?

Thus, Goda Devi is telling us all that it is essential to get up early and listen to the prayers of the Lord!

Pasuram:

పక్షులు కూసెను, ¹పక్షిరాట్పత్ర మం
　　దిర శంఖనాదమ్ము చొరదె చెవుల?
మెల్లగాలేచి మునితల్లజుల్ యోగులు
　　క్షీరాబ్ధిశాయిని శేషతల్ప
లోకనిర్మాతను లోకసంరక్షకు
　　కపటకాంతా స్తనగరల పాయి
శకటాసురధ్వంసి చరణవిక్రము మనో
　　నిలయుని కీర్తించు వినదమదిగో
హరి హరి హరి యంచు నాశాంతరాళమ్ము
లలమి మామకాంతరంగములను
పల్లవింప(జేసె పిల్లరో! ఇకనైన
నిదురలేచి రావె నీలవేణి!

¹పక్షిరాజు పత్ర – One who has the king of birds (Garuda) as His vehicle -Lord Vishnu

PASURAM 7

Goda Devi was trying to wake up another girl who had committed herself to do the ritual but still sleeping.

கீசு கீசென்று எங்கும் ஆனைச் சாத்தன் கலந்து
    பேசின பேச்சரவம் கேட்டிலையோ பேய்ப் பென்ணே
காசும் பிறப்பும் கலகலப்பக் கைபேர்த்து
    வாச நறுங்குழல் ஆய்ச்சியர் மத்தினால்
ஓசைப் படுத்த தயிர் அரவம் கேட்டிலையோ
    நாயகப் பெண் பிள்ளாய்! நாராயணன் மூர்த்தி
கேசவனைப் பாடவும் நீ கேட்டே கிடத்தியோ
    தேசமுடையாய்! திற ஏல் ஓர் எம்பாவாய்.

Keesu keesu enru engum aanaich chaaththaan kalandhu-

Paesina paechcharavam kaettilaiyo paeyp pennae

Kaasum pirappum kalakalappak kai paerththu

Vaasa narum kuzhal aaychchiyar maththinaal-

Osai paduththa thayiraravam kaettilaiyo

Naayagap pen pillaay naaraayanan moorththi

Kaesavanaip paadavum nee kaettae kidaththiyo

Dhaesamudaiyaay thiravaelor embaavaay (7)

Meaning: Oh! Lady! You have volunteered to lead us all in performing this Margashira Masam ritual. You mentioned that you would wake up early and then wake us all up since you told us that getting up early for the ritual is essential. Yet, how come you are still sleeping? Please get up quickly and join us for the ritual.

As the Geeta says,

यद्यदाचरति श्रेष्टः तत्तदेव इतरो जनः
स यत्प्रमाणम् कुरुते लोकस्तदनुवर्तते॥
(Geeta 3:21)

One who is a leader has to perform first, and others follow that path. Hence a good leader will be conscientious since people do not follow what he says but what he does.

As a leader, how do you expect others to get up early if you yourself do not get up early? Do not try to argue that it is not yet early morning. The Bharadvaaja birds are already flying to find their food and making 'kicha' 'kicha' sounds so loudly that everyone can hear. Did birds' sounds not reach your ears? Perhaps you have locked the door and covered yourself so much that you might not have heard those sounds. After performing their daily housekeeping activities, the matured Gopikas are now carrying the things to sell and coming into town. You may not see them as you have closed your eyes and are sleeping. The homemakers who got up early and are actively churning the curds for butter, and in the process, the ornaments on their necks and the marriage necklace are rubbing each other and making a lot of noise all over - could you not hear them? Usually, people do not have earlids like eyelids to open or close. By any chance, do you have earlids that you have closed so that you cannot hear at all these morning sounds?

In the process of churning, the body moves to the left and then to the right. Due to this, the decorations and flowers used during the night fall all over the house, and their smell spreads. Have you not at least smelled those by your nose, causing you to wake up?

కలవింటింటను గోవు లున్నయవి లేగల్ మాపటన్ వాని త ల్గుల బంధించెద రావులన్ బిదికి పాల్ గుంపట్లలో (గాతు రిం తులు వే(టోక యె లేచి చిల్కుదురు చేతుల్ సాచి యువ్పొ ంగు గు బ్బలు నర్తింపగ లేత [1]కౌనటమటింపన్ గాపుతల్ మజ్జిగన్|
(My Ramireddy book) - [1]నడుము.

Not only that, while churning the buttermilk, they were also singing the glories of the Lord, like how He destroyed the rakshasas or demons like Kesi, etc. Have you not heard those singings that could have helped you to get up? At least now, you should get up and set us an example by leading us all to do the ritual. Now please open your doors for that.

Goda Devi teaches all of us in a way that we should get up every day before sunrise and, after cleaning ourselves, perform the daily duties with the feeling that all these activities become rituals if we keep our minds on the Lord and, if possible, keep chanting his name, while performing the routine physical activities.

By singing the glories of the Lord or chanting the name of the Lord, reminding ourselves that even the body is functioning only because of His grace, our mind gets purified. It also prevents the mind from running into unnecessary self-centered activities and keeps the mind peaceful and serene. By His grace, the six enemies that bother the mind constantly, desire, anger, greediness, delusion, pride, and evilness – the six enemies will not enter our mind, thereby keeping it ready to serve the Lord, who is expressing Himself as the entire universe.

Pasuram:

నాయకురాలివై నాయమా నిదురింత
వేగెడిదాకను పిచ్చిపిల్ల
కీచుచీచు మటంచు నేచు నేత్రింతల
పలుకు లెల్లెడ బర్వె కలికి వినవె
కరకంకణమ్ము‌లు కంటెకాసులు తాళి
కలసి మ్రోయ(గ గొల్లనెలత లెల్ల
వలచు కొప్పులు గదల వాలు(గంటి! కేలు
కదలించి కవ్వాన(గడవ(తెరుగు
చిట్టుట్టు మటంచును చిలుకు చప్పు
డైన వినలేదో! వెల(ది! నారాయణావ
తారు కేశవు కీర్తన ధ్వనుల నేని?
తలుపు తీయవే ఇకనేని తలిరు(బో(డి!|

PASURAM 8

....

Introduction:

Goda Devi is trying to wake up another girl who expressed interest in performing the ritual.

கீழ்வானம் வெள்ளென்று எருமை சிறு வீடு
   மேய்வான் பரந்தன காண் மிக்குள்ள பிள்ளைகளும்
போவான் போகின்றாரைப் போகாமல் காத்து உன்னைக்
   கூவுவான் வந்து நின்றோம் கோதுகலமுடைய
பாவாய் எழுந்திராய் பாடிப் பறை கொண்டு
   மாவாய் பிளந்தானை மல்லரை மாட்டிய
தேவாதி தேவனைச் சென்று நாம் சேவித்தால்
   ஆவாவென்று ஆராய்ந்து அருள் ஏல் ஓர் எம்பாவாய்

Keezh vaanam vellenru erumai siru veedu

Maeyvaan parandhana kaan mikkulla pillaigalum

Povaan poginraaraip pogaamal kaaththu unnaik-

Koovuvaan vandhu ninrom kodhugalamudaiya-

Paavaay ezhundhiraay paadip parai kondu

Maavaay pilandhaanai mallarai maattiya

Dhaevaadhi dhaevanaich chenru naam saeviththaal

Aavaavenru aaraayndhu arulaelor embaavaay.

In the east, the sky is slowly getting clearer and brighter as it is becoming morning. Yet, how come you are still sleeping? The buffaloes that we think are dumb have already got up and left the backyard searching for their food. Our friends, who have committed to doing the ritual, are already on their way to take a bath in the river in preparation for the ritual. I stopped them, and we came together to wake you up. We have been waiting in front of your house for some time. We called you again and again, but you did not seem to respond as you were still sleeping. Our time is getting wasted. We want to use this time for singing the devotional songs to our heart's content on the Lord, who killed Aswaasura and the wrestlers, so that He may be pleased and bless us. Hence get up quickly and join us in taking a bath.

Explanation: Human beings are blessed with evolved intellect, unlike other living beings. Hence, by gaining this human birth, one must work for the four purusharthas – dharma, artha, kaama, and moksha; with artha (earning wealth) and kaama the desires to fulfill are bounded by dharma on one side, and with the goal of moksha on the other. The first three are for those who want to enjoy life. The evolved beings work to gain moksha, using God-given human birth. The do's and don'ts for human beings are prescribed in the Vedas to help them with their rapid evolution. Geeta says,

त्रैगुण्यविषया वेदा निस्त्रैगुण्यो भवार्जुन।
निर्द्वंद्वो नित्यसत्वस्थो निर्योग क्षेम आत्मवान्।
(Geeta 2:45)

The word त्रैगुण्य is used to indicate the human beings that have three gunas; satva, rajas, and tamo gunas. Vedas are meant to teach all of them.

यावानर्थ उदपाने सर्वतस्संप्लुतोदके।
तावान् सर्वेषु वेदेषु ब्राह्मणस्य विजानतः॥
(Geeta 2:46)

The water in the tank helps take baths, feed the cows and animals, fertilize the land, and even for someone committing suicide. However, one, who is thirsty, uses only that much water to quench his thirst and not more than that. In the same way, there is so much discussed in the Vedas. However, the seekers who want moksha study only those relevant portions for them and leave the rest with the help of a teacher.

The buffalo does not have the brains to think. Even though Lord has given them brains to think, some human beings do not use them properly or use them, morning to evening and from birth to death, only to fulfill their self-centered desires. Hence Goda Devi says, *'erumai siru veedu maeyvaan parandhana kaan'*, those intelligent beings who do not want to waste their life on sense-pleasures, try to get out of this cycle of birth and death by seeking the Lord's grace and perform His duties. Hence Prahalada in Bhagavatam says,

చక్రి చింత లేని జన్మంబు జన్మమే
తరళ సలిల బుద్బుదంబు గాక
విష్ణుభక్తి లేని విబుధుండు విబుధుడే
పాదయుగముతోడి పశువుగాక। (Potana)

Those who constantly think of the Lord are called vibhudas (devas in human form) or wise ones. Others, even though they may be scholars in objective sciences, are only two-legged animals as they cannot correctly use the brains that the Lord has given them to think of higher.

Hence Goda Devi says, we have stopped the ladies who are already on the way to serve the Lord and came here to take you also with us, so that you can also get the benefits of these prayers.. *'povaan poginraaraip pogaamal kaaththu unnaikkoovuvaan vandhu ninrom'*.

अनेकजन्म सहस्र तपोध्यान समधिभिः
जनानाम् क्षीणपापानाम् कृष्णे भक्तिः प्रजायते॥

To be blessed with supreme devotion to Lord Krishna requires merits earned in many past lives.

लोकाध्यक्षम् स्तुवन्नित्यम् सर्वदुःखातिगो भवेत्।

సంకీర్త్య నారాయణశబ్దమాత్రం విముక్త దుఃఖాః సుఖినో భవంతి।

नामस्मरणा दन्योपायम् नहि पश्यामो भवतरणे।
Thus, there are many sayings that glorify the effect of chanting the name of Lord Narayana. It will destroy all the miseries associated with samsara and provide everlasting peace everyone is longing for.

ध्यायन् कृते, यजन् यज्ञैः त्रेतायाम्, द्वापरेऽर्चयन्।
यदाप्नोति तदाप्नोति कलौ संकीर्त्य केशवम्।
(Vishnupuranam)

Hence in the kali yuga, singing the glories of the Lord is the means for moksha. Hence Goda Devi says: '*maavaay pilandhaanai mallarai maattiya dhaevaadhi dhaevanaich chenru naam saeviththaal*'.

When a rakshasa by the name Keshi took the form of a human being and joined the crowd and was making a havoc,

భీషణ ఘోటక దానవ
హేషానిర్ఘోషభిన్న హృదయ నిఖిల గో
యోషా పురుషార్భకమై
ఘోషము హరిసూడ దైన్యఘోషం టయ్యెన్| (Potana)

Thus, one who is making havoc in the town (Krisha) Krishna threw him away. But when he returned with a vengeance, Krishna entered his stomach and grew up so big that the demon's stomach busted, thereby killing him.

వాయువు వెడలక నిలిచిన(
గాయంటు సెమర్ప(గన్ను(గవ వెలికుఱికన్
మాయసెడి తన్ను కొనుచును
కూయుచునశ్వాసురుండు గూలెన్ నేలన్|

ఘోటకాసురేంద్రు కుక్షిలో(గృష్ణుని
బాహువధికమైన(బట్టలేమి(
టగలి దోసపండు పగిది(తద్దేహంటు
వసుమతీశ! రెండు వ్రక్కలయ్యె| (Potana)

Thus Krishna, who killed Keshi and Mullaras. Kamsa instigated Chanuura to kill the cowherds, Krishna and Balarama, in a dual fight.

హరికిని లో(టడి తెగడక
హరియురమ్ము మహో(hO)గ్ర ముష్టి నహితు(డు పొడువన్
హరి కుసుమ మాలికాహత
కరిభంగి(టరాక్రమించె(గలహోద్ధతు(డై||

శౌరి సెటి(జొచ్చి కరములు
క్రూరగతిన్ బట్టి త్రిప్పి కుంభిని వైచెన్
శూరున్ గలహగభీరున్
వీరున్ చాణూరు ఘోరు వితతాకారున్|

శోణితము నేర నోలుక(గ(
జాణూరుండడ్లు కృష్ణసంబ్రామణ సం
క్షీణుండై క్షీణింటడి
ప్రాణంటులు విడిచె(గంసు ప్రాణము గల(గన్|

అంత   నద్దనుజాంతకుండు   చరణప్రహరణంటుల
భిన్న మస్తకులం జేసి వాని చెలులం గూటతో సలశలుల
నంతకాంతికంటున కనిచిన – (From Potana)

Thus by serving the Lord who is born to protect the good and punish the evil.

'aavaavenru aaraayndhu arulaelor', he will listen to our prayers and bless us with compassion. If we become eligible for His blessings by giving up all our desires to enjoy sense-pleasures, and only desire His abode, He will take us to His fold and protect us.

To deserve that, we should have single-pointed devotion towards Him, without any other dissipating thoughts, with the minds fully involved desiring only His grace, and completely surrender ourselves at His holly feet – then, as Krishna says,

अनन्याश्चिंतयन्तो माम् ये जनाः पर्युपासते
तेषाम् नित्याभियुक्तानाम् योगक्षेमम् वहाम्यहम्।
(Geeta 9:22)

thus He promised to take care of us fully and completely, providing whatever He thinks we need. Protection does not mean not just worldly comforts, which others can give, but giving us the His highest abode, which is the very purpose of life itself that others cannot give.

ఇత్తురుగాక నిర్ఝర సురేశ గిరీశ సరస్వతీశులన్।
దత్తడి(టుత్తడిన్ సుతుల దారల భూముల వాహగేహ సం
పత్తుల, దానపాటవము వారల కెవ్వని వల్ల కల్గె
లోకోత్తరు గొల్తు నా హరి ననుత్తమ ముక్తిదు మా
మనోహరున్। (My Shantivilasamu)

నిరువధి సౌఖ్యదాయక మనిందిత మవ్యయమైన మోక్షమే
నరునకు రక్షణమ్మన, జనార్దను వీడి మరొక్క దైవ మే
కరణి నొసంగ నోపును? జగజ్జననాదుల కర్తయైన యా
వరుడు నిరంజనుండు నిరుపాధికబంధువు జీవకోటికిన్।।
(My Yatirajiyamu)

Thus, by serving the Lord Narayana only, we can get what we do not have, and He removes what we do not need. What we need ultimately is moksha that He alone can give us.

अग्निज्योतिरहः शुक्लः षण्मासा उत्तरायणम्
तत्र प्रयाता गच्छति ब्रह्म ब्रह्मविदो जनाः| (Geeta)

Thus, avoiding regular difficult paths involving lokas after lokas, He will take us directly on His Garuda to His paramdhaama or supreme abode. Hence Goda Devi says, Oh! Girl! 'kodhugalamudaiya paavaay', even though desirous of serving the Lord of the universe and wanted to join us in this ritual, how come you are still sleeping! 'ezhundhiraay!' at least get up now and join us in the ritual. Before all our friends leave, let us join them to do the Margasira ritual.

Pasuram:

తెల్లవారెను తూర్పుదెసనింగి, యెనుములు
　　వెలికి బోయెను మేయ(తెరడు వీడి,
పో(బోవు పిల్లలు(బోనీక నిలిపెన్
　　బిలువ వచ్చితి మేము పెంకిపిల్ల,
నీ యింటి ముంగిట నిలిచియున్నా మొసి
　　లెమ్ము వే రమ్ము గానమ్ము సేయ
మాపురూపుని సొకు మర్దించి మల్లుర
　　హాతమార్చి నట్టి దేవాధిదేవు
చేత డిక్కిటూని చిత్తము తత్పాద
యుగలమందు(జేర్చి నిగమగమ్ము
హరి నుతింప మనల నాదరించును దయా
రస తరంగితాంతరంగమునను.

PASURAM 9

Introduction:

Goda Devi is waking up a girl who happened to be very wealthy.

தூமணி மாடத்துச் சுற்றும் விளக்கெரிய
    தூபம் கமழ துயில் அணை மேல் கண் வளரும்
மாமான் மகளே! மணிக்கதவம் தாள் திறவாய்!
    மாமீர்! அவளை எழுப்பீரோ? உம் மகள் தான்
ஊமையோ அன்றிச் செவிடோ அனந்தலோ
    ஏமப் பெருந்துயில் மந்திரப்பட்டாளோ?
மாமாயன் மாதவன் வைகுந்தன் என்றென்று
    நாமம் பலவும் நவின்று ஏல் ஓர் எம்பாவாய்

Thoomani maadaththu sutrum vilakkeriyath

Thoopam kamazhath thuyilanaimael kan valarum

Maamaan magalae manik kadhavam thaazh thiravaay

Maameer avalai ezhuppeero un magal thaan-

Oomaiyo anri sevido ananthalo

Aemap perunn thuyil mandhirap pattaalo

Maamaayan maadhavan vaikundhan enrenru

Naaman palavum navinraelor embaavaay (9)

Meaning: Oh! Uncle's daughter! What a girl you are! You told us you would come with us to take a holy bath in the river before doing puja. How come you are still sleeping and have not gotten up yet? How can you get up early, as you are sleeping in a diamond-fitted house, with a glistening variety of lights due to all the diamonds around you, sleeping on a luxurious soft bed made of the finest soft feathers of Hamsa/swan, and having sweet dreams? We all came and stood in front of your house and called you. At least for now, you can get up. Please open your diamond-fitted doors. Since you are still not getting up, I am calling your mother. Aunty! Please wake up your daughter. She is not getting up when we are all calling. Are you listening? Did you hear our request? She is only your daughter and seems to have acquired your qualities. Is she sleeping, or have you made a rule that nobody should wake her up? Did you arrange a security guard in front of her chamber so that no one would disturb her sleep? Or have you put some magic spell, so she does not get up? We are singing so loud the glories of the most magical person, the Lord of Vaikunta, the husband of Ramaa Devi. Even after listening to these divine songs, she is still sleeping. What kind of girl is your daughter?

Explanation:

Wealth can contribute to arrogance and thus take us away from the Lord. One must experience the pleasures and comforts to the degree that Lord has bestowed on us. However, desperately depending on wealth or luxuries will make us become a slave to them. One should experience these as though it is His prasad or gift for us, with a reverential attitude, and share these with those who are less fortunate. Hence one devotee asks for 'विपदस्सन्तु वश्यश्वद्यासु संकीर्त्यते हरिः' | Oh! Lord, give us a lot of problems so that our minds will keep thinking of you. People think of the Lord when they are in trouble, not when they are happy. Kunti Devi also asked the same. She asked Krishna,

विपदः संतु ताः सस्वत् शाश्वत् तत्र तत्र जगद्गुरो|
भवतो दर्शनम् यत् स्याद् अपुनर्भव दर्शनम्|

'I wish that all those calamities would happen again and again so that we could see You again and again, for seeing You means that we will no longer see repeated births and deaths.' (Srimad-Bhagavatam 1.8.25)Krishna says in Geeta about four types of Bhaktas,

चतुर्विधा भजन्ते माम् जनास्सुकृतिनोर्जुन|
आर्तो जिज्ञासु रर्थार्थी ज्ञानी च भरतर्षभ||
(Geeta 7:16)

Some people think of God only when they are desperate; otherwise, not. Some are just curious to know about God. Some think of God whenever they need something. These people go to temples with a long list of what they want. Some are not interested to learn about the greatness of the Lord. They only think and pray to God when the troubles become unbearable.

Kulashekhara Alwar says, यद्यद्द्रव्यम् भवतु भगवन् पूर्वकर्मानुरूपम् , whatever that comes in life is due to our actions in the past, whether they are pleasures or pains. Every action will have its result. Pandavas, although close friends of Krishna, had to suffer greatly due to their past karmas. However, these difficulties only helped Pandavas refine themselves and made them better at dealing with Kauravas.

Hence it is best to know first the source of pleasures and pains that contribute to our suffering, life after life, and only request for the means for liberation that involves complete surrender to the Lord of the universe, Sreeman Narayana. Krishna says a wise person accepts whatever comes due to prarabhda karmas.

दुःखेषु अनुद्विग्नमनाः सुखेषु विगतस्पृहः
वीतरागभयक्रोधः स्थितधीर्मुनिरुच्यते॥
(Geeta 2:56)

The wise person will not get perturbed when the sufferings come or not get elated when the pleasures come due to their praarabda since his mind is reveling in the supreme reality.

Excess sleep more than the body needs is due to tamoguna. One goes from tamas to rajas to satvik in on evolutionary ladder.

तमस्त्वज्ञानजम् विद्धि मोहनम् सर्वदेहिनाम्।
प्रमादालस्य निद्राभिस्तन्निबध्नाति भारत।
(Geeta 14:8).

Those, who are deluded and fond of their bodies and sense pleasures, have predominantly Tamo guna, arising from the lack of understanding of their true nature. It contributes to laziness and sleepiness and creates dangerous situations for them. Hence one must control these and slowly evolve to gain rajas and then sattva gunas.

Goda Devi says, *'sutrum vilakkeriyath'*, the lights are burning around. They will only remove the outside darkness but cannot remove inner darkness due to ignorance of one's own self. The enchanting smells outside, luxuries, soft beds to sleep on, etc., make us more dependent on external comforts. These make us slaves to them and only take our minds away from the Lord. Bharthruhari says (Telugu translation by Enugu Lakshmana Kavi)

ఒకచో నేలను తవ్వళించు, నొకచో నొప్పారు౯ టూసెజ్జ పై,
నొకచో శాకము లారగించు, నొకచో నుత్కృష్టశాల్యోదనం,
టొకచో౯ టొంత ధరించు, నొక్కొక తటిన యోగ్యాంటర శ్రేణి, లె
క్కకు రానీయcడు కార్య సాధకుcడు దుఃఖంటున సుఖంటున
మదిన్!!

'He may sleep on the floor, or on a soft flowery bed, eat minimum food, or eat in luxurious full course meal, cover himself with bare minimum or ware decorative dress, etc. He does not care about the pleasures and pains in life when he is fully committed to doing what needs to be done.'

The knowledgeable seekers do not long for these external comforts and only desire to please the Lord through dharmic actions and prayers. Hence in these Kaliyuga-times, glorifying the name of the Lord is the best approach to reaching him. 'नामस्मरणा दन्योपायम् नहि पश्यामो भवतरणे'. Hence, we should spend our time singing the glories of Lord Narayana, the husband of Lakshmi, whose abode is Vaikunta. The Lord is the master of maaya too and waits to ensure our devotion is sincere.

The whole Prakriti itself is the expression of His maaya. The maaya can cause temptation for sense indulgence and thus cause delusion to the Jeeves. The only way to get out of the clutches of maaya is to surrender ourselves to the Lord of maaya, Sreeman Narayana. Krishna says in Geeta,

दैवी ह्येषाम् गुणमयी मम माया दुरत्यया।
मामेवये प्रपद्‌यंते मायामेताम् तरंति ते॥ (Geeta 7:14)

This maaya of mine is of divine origin, and it is difficult to cross it by self-effort. Only by surrendering to Me one can cross this maaya and reach Me. This Prakriti is maaya – मायंतु प्रकृतिम् विद्‌यात् – says Swetasvatara Upanishat. It is also called Parameswara shakti, or the power of the Lord. A Jeeva can get caught in the clutches of this maaya and gets bound and goes through life after life. One cannot easily get out of this. The only way to get out is to surrender oneself completely and fully with full devotion to the Lord.

Hence Goda Devi says, Oh! Darling daughter of my uncle, please get up soon. Come quickly and join us in the Margasira ritual.

Pasuram:

మాణిక్య భవనాన మణిదీపికలు వెల్గ
   కమ్మని ధూపమ్ము క్రమ్ముకొన(గ
మెత్తని పాన్పుపై మెయిసేర్చి, కన్ను మూ
   సిన మామ కూ(తురా! చిన్నెలాడి!
వచ్చి తీయవే మణి వాకిలి తలుపుల
   గడియ, నీ యిల్లు బంగారుగాను
అత్త! లేపగ రాదె, యామెను నీవైన?
   నీ కూతురే గదా! నిద్రలోన
మునిగియన్నదె? చెవిటియా? మూగ? మంత్ర
ముగ్ధయా? గుప్తయా? మేము మురవిరోధి
మాధవుని విష్ణు వైకుంతు మాయలాని
పలుదెఱంగుల(బాడినా పలుకదేల?

PASURAM 10

Introduction:

Goda Devi is trying to wake up another girl who committed herself to join the ritual but is still sleeping.

நோற்றுச் சுவர்க்கம் புகுகின்ற அம்மனாய்!
மாற்றமும் தாராரோ வாசல் திறவாதார்
நாற்றத் துழாய் முடி நாராயணன் நம்மால்
போற்றப் பறை தரும் புண்ணியனால் பண்டு ஒரு
நாள்
கூற்றத்தின் வாய் வீழ்ந்த கும்பகருணனும்
தோற்று முனக்கே பெருந்துயில்தான் தந்தானோ?
ஆற்ற அனந்தலுடையாய் அருங்கலமே
தேற்றமாய் வந்து திற ஏல் ஓர் எம்பாவாய்!

Notruch chuvarkkam puguginra ammanaay!

Maatramum thaaraaro vaasal thiravaadhaar

Naatrath thuzhaay mudi naaraayanan nammaal

Potrap parai tharum punniyanaal pandu oru naal

Kootraththin vaay veezhndha kumbakarananum

Thotrum unakkae perunthuyil thaan thandhaano

Aatra anandhal udaiyaay arungalamae

Thaetramaay vandhu thiravaelor embaavaay (10)

Meaning: Due to performance of many merits and blessed with luxurious life as a result, Oh! Meritorious lady, even if you do not want to open the doors, can you at least respond to us? Do you think the pearls will fall out of your mouth by talking to us? The one who decorates himself with a garland of Tulasi leaves, Shreeman Narayana, blessed us with many comforts and luxuries due to our prayers in the past. But these comforts and pleasures will not take us to our final destiny. For that, we need to surrender ourselves to Him completely.

Instead of coming with us to serve him, how come you are still sleeping? You seem to be addicted to that. Even Kumbhakarna, who is very fond of sleeping, will lose in competition with you in sleeping. When he died at the hands of Lord Rama, did he pass his sleep habits to you? If you keep doing this, you will bring great glory to your families, your father's and your husband's sides! Enough of your sleep. Please get up and open the doors for us.

Explanation:

మేలు చేసెనేని మేలొందు మనుజుండు
కీడుచేసెనేని కీడు గుడుచు
తనదు కర్మఫలము తా(బొందవలె(గాక
దాని నితరు(దెవడు తలభరించు. (My Sudhabinduvulu)

If we are enjoying life now, it is only due to merits earned due to our prayers in the past life. If we want to enjoy our future lives, then we have to earn merits in this life. Hence, we should not stop our prayers thinking that these pleasures will continue forever.

However, once we have learned the fundamental cause of our cycle of births and deaths, we recognize these temporary pleasures in life are not worth the effort. They will only keep us in bondage. At last, we have come to the stage as human beings endowed with intelligence. Hence, we must use this rare opportunity and work towards our permanent solvation.

One who works towards the highest goal should constantly think about how to secure everlasting happiness without getting lost in the fleeting sense-pleasures, '*naatrath thuzhaay mudi naaraayanan*'.

Why is He worried about all these Jeevas when other Gods do not bother about them? If one asks, He is none other than Lord Narayana Himself. He is called Narayana, meaning He is the very goal for all naras or human beings. He is a true savior and solace to everybody. Moreover,

पिता च रक्षक श्शेषी भर्ता ञेयो रमापतिः।
स्वाम्याधारो ममात्मा च भोक्ता चाद्यमनूदितः

Thus, He relates himself to human beings in many ways. The physical bodies are made up of five fundamental gross elements into which Jeeva enters to exhaust his kamas. The Lord himself creates these elements. He ensures that the Jeevas enter the appropriate bodies needed to exhaust their karmas. Thus, eighty-five thousand varieties of living beings on this earth itself, and many more in the fourteen worlds he controls at that scale.

.....मे भिन्ना प्रकृतिरष्टधा।
अपरेय मितस्त्वन्याम् प्रकृतिम् विद्धि मे पराम्।
जीवभूताम् महाबाहो ययेदम् धार्यते जगत्।
ए तद्योनीनि भूतानि सर्वाणीत्युपधारय।
(Geeta 6-7:4)

The Universe is formed by Bhagavan's para and aparaa Prakruti.

'अहम् कृत्स्नस्य जगतः प्रभवः प्रलयस्तथा। says Krishna in Geeta (7:6).

Hence Lord Narayana is the father of this entire universe. He is also the protector of all Jeevas and the Universe, as they are all part of His creation. Protector also means He is the one who gives the moksha to the deserving Jeevas. Hence Krishna says,

ममैवांशो जीवलोके जीवभूतस्सनातनः Geeta (15:7)

Since all Jeeves are part of Him (shesha bhutas), He is the support for all by saying that "स्त्री प्राय मितरं जगत्, the whole universe can be considered as a wife and since He is the only Purusha, He is called Bharta – the one who supports. The whole Prakruti is the symbol of Lakshmi, and He is called Lakshmi pati or the husband of Lakshmi. Thus, Prakriti and Purusha are symbolic of Laksmi Narayana.

If we know the root of anything, we know, in essence, the whole thing. If we know Lord Narayana, we as well know the whole universe. A student of Upanishad goes to his teacher and asks 'कस्मिन्नु भगोवो विज्ञाते सर्वम् इदम् विज्ञातुम् भवति', Sir, please teach me knowing which I will know everything (Mudaka Upanishad). And the teacher was delighted that the student was interested in learning the essence of the whole universe. He taught para and apara Prakruti and the substratum of all, Brahman or Lord Narayana, knowing whom one, in essence, knows everything.

Since the whole world is formed by the Leela of Lord Narayana, it is called Leela vibhuti. Purusha suuktam says this is only one forth of His creation, and the other threeforth is called divya vibhuti – 'पादोश्य विश्वाभूतानि, त्रिपादस्य अमृतम् दिवि'.

पश्यंतीषु श्रुतिषु परितः सूरिबृंदेन साऋम्
मध्येकृत्य त्रिगुणफलकम् निर्मितस्थानभेधम्,
विश्वाधीशप्रणयिनिः सदा विभ्रमद्यूतवृत्तौ
ब्रह्मेशाद्या दधति युवयोरक्षशारप्रचारम्|| (Shree Stuti of Vedantadeshika)

సరసిజసూతి శంకరుడు శుక్రు(డు
మున్నుగ దేవజాతులున్
నరులును నీడజ ప్రభృతి నైక
చరిష్ణువులెల్ల(గాయలె
పరచిన పట్టమై ప్రకృతి వర్తిల,
సూరులు చూచుచుండగా
హరి సిరి(గూడి పాచికల నాడుట
లౌదట లోకవృత్తముల్| (My Yatirajeyam)

Thus, He is the controller and the Lord of both para and apara Prakriti. Jeeva is part of Him only.

Without Jeeva present in the body, it will stand or walk. The body becomes a vehicle for the Jeeva to transact in the world. For that Jeeva, however, the Lord is the innermost self, supporting him. Without His support, Jeeva cannot do anything.

यस्यात्मा शरीरम् - says shruti. वासुदेवात्म कान्याहुः (Bhaaratam)

क्षेत्रम् क्षेत्रज् एवच - Geeta

Hence these statements show that He is the very soul of all beings.

भोक्ता च प्रभुरेवच' - says Geeta.

Since He is the creator of this entire phenomenal world as His 'leela vibhuti' – He is also Bhoktaa, the enjoyer of the world.

Thus, He has a nine-fold relationship with the world. He became 'ayanam' or shelter for the world of beings. He likes 'Tulasi' very much. He will be pleased if we worship Him with Tulasi leaves. In India, people keep the Tulasi plants in front of their houses. By worshiping Him, our dharmic desires also will be fulfilled. Hence Goda Devi says, this is the best time for worship, and it is not good that you are still sleeping. Sleep is a sign of Tamo guna. Those who are engulfed by Tamo guna, physically, however strong they are, ultimately end up losing. The well-known children's story of the race between squirrel and tortoise, where the squirrel lost the race because of Tamo guna. The story of Kumbhakarna is another example. Even after gaining the boons from Brahmaji, and becoming a terror for many opponents, yet ultimately succumbed to the God of Death.

Goda Devi says, Oh! Girl! You seem to outperform even Kumbhakarna in sleep. Has he gifted you with his sleep when he left his body? It is time now. Please get up and open the door and join us in the ritual. If not, at least respond to our calls. Are you lazy even to answer us? That is not proper. At least open the door for us.

Pasuram:

పలునోములను నోచి పడసిన స్వర్గ సౌ
	ఖ్యాంబుధి మునిగిన యతివమిన్న,
తెరువకున్నను తల్పు తెరవరో నోరైన(
	దెరచిన ముత్తెము లురలు నేమె?
నుతియింప నారాయణుని తులసీ ధారి
	అర్థమ్ము లిచ్చు పుణ్యమ్ము కొలది
కూలుచు జమువాత కుంభకర్ణుడు పందె
	మోడి నిద్దుర నీకు నొసగి చనెనొ?
గొల్ల తలిరుబోండ్ల కెల్ల నలంకార
	మైనదాన, తెర కట్టు నేమె
సుఖము? నిద్ర దేరి శోభనాంగీ మణి
	లెమ్ము తలుపుతీయ రమ్ము వేగ.

PASURAM 11

Introduction:

Goda Devi is trying to wake-up another girl, who is very proud of her beauty, who committed to join in performing the ritual but perhaps spent her time in trying to beautify herself and now not able to get up.

கற்றுக் கறவைக் கணங்கள் பல கறந்து
   செற்றார் திறல் அழியச் சென்று செருச் செய்யும்
குற்ற மொன்றில்லாத கோவலர் தம் பொற்கொடியே
   புற்று அரவு அல்குல் புனமயிலே போதராய்
சுற்றத்துத் தோழிமார் எல்லோரும் வந்து நின்
   முற்றம் புகுந்து முகில் வண்ணன் பேர் பாட
சிற்றாதே பேசாதே செல்வப் பெண்டாட்டி நீ
   எற்றுக்கு உறங்கும் பொருள் ஏல் ஓர் எம்பாவாய்!

Katruk karavaik kanangal pala karandhu

Setraar thiralazhiyach chenru seruch cheyyum

Kutram onrillaadha kovalartham porkodiyae

Putru aravu alkul punamayilae podharaay

Sutraththu thozhimaar ellaarum vandhu nin-

Mutram pugundhu mugil vannan paer paada

Sitraadhae paesaadhae selva pendaatti nee-

Etrukku urangum porulaelor embaavaay (11)

Meaning: Oh! Beautiful damsel! You have not yet gotten up from your sleep! You come from a tradition where people are very conscious of their duties. They get up early and are already busy milking the cows, taking care of them, helping their friends, punishing the enemies, etc. Thus, they are already doing their assigned duties. Coming from such duty-bound families, how come you are still sleeping? You have committed to joining us in the ritual, yet you are still sleeping. We have come and waiting at your doorstep. While waiting, we are all singing the glories of the Lord, and yet you are pretending to sleep. Do you want to join us in this ritual or not? Let us know what you want to do. Oh! Beautiful girl with delicate skin and long hair. Do you think our darling Lord Krishna who loves beauty, will come rushing, falling for your beauty?

Explanation: There is a close association between the clouds in the sky and the peacocks. They spread their wings and dance when the external weather is conducive for them.

मेघ पर्वतयो रब्धि चंद्रयोरब्ज सूर्ययो:
शिखिजीमूतयोर्दृष्टिरम्य योर्मित्रता स्वयम्‌|

Lord is set to be blue. Blue indicates infiniteness. The vast oceans or limitless sky looks blue. Hence Lord is called neelameghasyaama – has a color resembling the dark clouds in the sky. This lady is 'punamayilae' like a forest, wild peacock. When the clouds are spread, the peacocks open their wings and dance around. It is their nature. When we are loudly singing the glories of the

Lord whose color is like heavy clouds, you who look like a peacock sleeping instead of jumping with joy; that is not fair.

The clouds do not think we have already rained here; why should we rain here again? In the same way, Lord Krishna will pour out his compassionate rains again and again on those who depend on Him. Someone may complain that He is showing His compassion to those who have surrendered to Him without thinking twice about their backgrounds, etc. It will violate His equanimity, affecting His Leela vibhuti. That thinking shows his lack of understanding of divine grace. Lord is equal to everybody who asks for His protection. He only would not bother those who do not ask for it. He will wait until they ask. Eventually, they will ask once they realize they cannot cross this ocean of samsara without surrendering completely to Him.

He says that He is equally compassionate to all, but those who surrender, I reciprocate their love. Thus He says,

समोहम् सर्व भूतेषु न मे द्वेष्योस्ति न प्रियः
ये भजंति तु माम् भक्त्या मयि ते तेषु चाप्यहम्॥
(Geeta 29-9).

However, whoever offers himself completely by surrendering to Me, I will take care of him completely. That is His promise.

अनन्याश्चिंतयन्तो माम् ये जनाः पर्युपासते|
तेषाम् नित्याभियुक्तानाम् योगक्षेमम् वहाम्यहम्||
(Geeta 9:22)

Hence, whoever gives up all their efforts and surrenders completely to Me, offering all their services to Me, I will relieve them from their karmas and provide the liberation they are longing for. And this constitutes His final teaching in Geeta (charama slokam).

सर्वधर्मान् परित्यज्य माम् एकम् शरणम् व्रज|
अहम् त्वाम् सर्वपापेभ्यो मोक्ष यिष्यामि मा शुचः
(Geeta 18:66)

సర్వధర్మములను సన్యసింపుము నాదు
చరణ కమలములను శరణు చొరుము
కాచువాడ నిన్ను కలుషంటు లన్నింటి
నడచి, యింక నీకు నడలు వలదు|| (My Yatirajeyamu)

Here, sarva dharmas mean all the previous paths that the Lord discussed before, to help to gain moksha. These include Jnaana, Karma, and Bhakti paths that He has discussed in the earlier chapters. One must give up all these since they are very difficult to accomplish for many. By following them, one can gain moksha, but following those paths involve a very diligent approach, and one cannot violate any rules, which is difficult to fulfill for many. In addition, if one surrenders to other Gods thinking it is easier, that will help only in gaining a lot of things except moksha, since other gods cannot give a seeker moksha.

Hence, Krishna says one must give up everything, and without any doubts and with a firm conviction, surrenders to Lord Narayana, to secure moksha. When seekers offer themselves completely, they will be blessed with the liberation they have longed for. In the process of surrendering, one should avoid all the actions that the Lord does not like (adharmic actions) and only do what pleases the Lord (by being compassionate to all and performing all His duties); then He will wipe out all the sins and give us the liberation; that is His promise.

The Gajendra, as long as he thought he could win over the crocodile by his self-effort, the Lord did not come to his rescue. Only when he realized that he could not save himself from that crocodile by his strength, he thought that only Lord could help him and no one else; hence he surrendered to the Lord.

లా వొక్కింతయు లేదు ధైర్యము
    విలోలంబయ్యె(బ్రాణంబులున్
రావుల్ దప్పెను, మూర్చవచ్చె(
    దనువున్ డస్సెన్ శ్రమంబయ్యెడిన్
నీవే తప్ప నితఃపరంబెఱు(గ
    మన్నింపన్ దగున్ దీనునిన్
రావే యీశ్వర కావవే వరద
    సంరక్షింపు భద్రాత్మకా|| (Potana)

Thus, when Gajendra gave up his fight for life, recognizing his inability to overcome his enemy, he surrendered completely to the Lord, requesting him, and praying that He is the only solace for him. As promised the Lord

సిరికిన్ జెప్పడు శంఖచక్రయుగముస్ జేదోయి సంధింప(డే
పరివారంబుస్ జీర(డభ్రగపతిస్ మన్నింప డాకర్ణికాం
తరధమ్మిల్ల ము(జక్క నొత్తడు వివాదప్రోత్థిత శ్రీకుచో
పరిచేలాంచలమైన వీడ(డు గజప్రాణావనోత్సాహియై||
(Potana)

The Lord Narayana leaving everything came running to protect Gajendra.

Hence Goda Devis says, if we serve Him with single pointed complete devotion, He will be pleased. Hence, she calls, Oh! Pretty girl! Do not think that I am a beautiful lady, and He will come running to me out of love for me. He looks for only inner beauty. Hence, it is time for you to get up and join us in this ritual as you originally wanted.

Moreover, you are born into a family of cowherds who are very conscious of their duties. By the by, the son of Nanda loves taking care of cows. You should follow your family tradition. Hence getting up early and doing your assigned duties is what Lord likes. Born to such a noble family, you must perform the duties that are favorable to the Lord. Instead, out of arrogance, if you neglect your duties, you only bring a bad name to your family. Hence, I urge you to get up quickly and join us in the prayers.

Pasuram:

కడవల కొలది లేగటియాల కదువుల
　　విసువక పాలను పిండి పిండి
బవరాన తెగ నీల్గు పగవారి బలముల
　　చేతుల తీ(టవో చండి చండి
కుటిల మింతయులేని గొల్లల కులము రం
　　గారు మేలైన టంగారు తీవ
భుజగమ్ము భోగమ్ము బోలు మల్గులదాన
　　వనమయూరము వంటి వన్నెలా(డి
తోడివా రెల్లరును గూడిమాడి యింటి
ముంగిటను జేరియున్నారు మొగిలు వన్నె
కాని(, బొగడుచు(బలుకవు కదలవిట్లు
పండి యుండగ నేల సంపన్నురాల?|

PASURAM 12

Goda Devi is trying to wake up another rich girl who committed to joining the ritual but is still sleeping.

கனைத்திளங் கற்றெருமை கன்றுக் கிறங்கி
நினைத்து முலை வழியே நின்று பால் சோர
நனைத்து இல்லம் சேறாக்கும் நற்செல்வன் தங்காய்
பனித்தலை வீழ நின் வாசல் கடை பற்றி
சினத்தினால் தென்னிலங்கைக் கோமானைச் செற்ற
மனத்துக்கு இனியானைப் பாடவும் நீ வாய் திறவாய்
இனித்தான் எழுந்திராய் ஈதென்ன பேருறக்கம்
அனைத்து இல்லத்தாரும் அறிந்து ஏல் ஓர்
எம்பாவாய்கனைத்திளங் கற்றெருமை கன்றுக்
கிறங்கி
நினைத்து முலை வழியே நின்று பால் சோர
நனைத்து இல்லம் சேறாக்கும் நற்செல்வன் தங்காய்
பனித்தலை வீழ நின் வாசல் கடை பற்றி
சினத்தினால் தென்னிலங்கைக் கோமானைச் செற்ற
மனத்துக்கு இனியானைப் பாடவும் நீ வாய் திறவாய்
இனித்தான் எழுந்திராய் ஈதென்ன பேருறக்கம்
அனைத்து இல்லத்தாரும் அறிந்து ஏல் ஓர்
எம்பாவாய்

Kanaiththu ilam katrerumai kanrukku irangi

Ninaiththu mulai vazhiyae ninru paal sora

Nanaiththu illam saeraakkum nar chelvan thangaay

Panith thalai veezha nin vaasar kadai patrich

Chinaththinaal then ilangaik komaanaich chetra

Manaththukku iniyaanaip paadavum nee vaay thiravaay

Iniththaan ezhundhiraay eedhenna paer urakkam

Anaiththu illaththaarum arindhaelor embaavaay (12)

Meaning: Oh! Rich Girl! What can we say about your enormous wealth? When hungry, the little calves call their mother cows 'Ambaa'. Their mothers come running, even breaking their tying ropes, to feed their babies out of love. Due to the stamping of the cows, their overflowing milk, and pouring rains, your front yard has become very muddy. You may be sleeping inside in a comfortable bed, but we are standing here in this muddy front yard as the rain is pouring down on our heads. We are not just standing but thinking of the Lord who took the incarnation of Vibhava. On the pretext that Ravana kidnapped his wife, Sita, the Lord built a **bridge** across the ocean and crossed it to reach Lanka with His army. He fought with Ravana and killed him. In addition, he blessed many sages who were praying for the Lord and had been persecuted before by Ravana.

Thus, we are standing in front of your house and praising the Lord in the form of Shree Ramachandra. Even after seeing us standing here and listening to our prayers to Lord Rama, you are still lying down and sleeping on your bed. What kind of sleep is yours? At least get up now, open the door, and join us in the prayers.

Implied meaning: Here, Goda Devi imagines that all the Jeeves are like calves crying for the Lord, who is the mother of the whole creation, for protection and enlightenment.

The cows, tied by ropes to the poles, become restless when they hear their calves calling for food. Thinking that these little calves do not have the strength to break open their ties and come to their mothers for their milk, and out of compassion for their babies, they came running with their overflowing milk to feed their calves. In the same way, the Lord, recognizing that His children cannot break their ties to the Prakruti and immersed deeply in this ocean of suffering and crying for help, out of compassion, takes birth in various forms to help them and relieve their pains.

In support of the Jeevas, He has created the five great elements. For shelter and support, the mother earth, water for drinking, air to breathe, fire to cook food, and space to move around. He brought the Jeevas from the stage of plants to insects, to birds to human forms, and blessed them with the adequate sense organs and intelligence to differentiate between right and wrong. He also provided Vedas that provide instructions on what is right and what is the wrong path and the consequences of following the wrong paths.

One can argue: These are all external things. They only provide food and comfort to the body, not to the soul. Helping to break the bonds of the Prakruti is useful. What kind of compassion is it in providing sense objects that bind us more and more by enjoying and getting us deeper into the bondage of Samsara? He should have provided us an aversion to these and helped us get out of this samsara rather than get us deeper into the bondage – is this not deceptive help? Is it like Shakuni in Mahabharata, who wants to destroy the Kuru dynasty by acting very friendly to Kauravas? Giving houses for shelter and tempting us by providing abundant materials things to enjoy – how can all this be considered helpful for the Jeevas? How can you call Him a compassionate one? If He is really compassionate, He should have given us an aversion to these so that our minds get tuned to higher than trying to indulge in them. One may ask.

Blessing all the Jeevas indiscriminately and giving all of them liberation is against the foundation of His Leela Vibhuti. That violates the very purpose of creation itself. Thinking of the safety and healthy growth of the babies, the mothers, out of compassion, feed the children with the requisite milk and other items, make them sleep, and play with them to make them happy, etc. However, as the children become adults, will the mothers continue to do the same things they did when they were babies? As the saying goes, when we become adults, even mothers will not give unless one requests.

In the same way, until the Jeevas become mature enough to discriminate between good and evil, the Lord takes care of them. However, just like the young man who wants to live independently and control his life, free from his parental pressures, the parents should only stand back and advise what is good and bad for the son to decide and live happily. They will stand back and observe and warn them if they go on the wrong path. Egoistically, Jeevas decide, either out of arrogance or out of passion, to go after sense objects; the Lord stands apart and waits until they ask for His help.

द्वा सुपर्णा सयुजा सखाया, समानम् वृक्षम् परिषस्वजाते।
तयोरन्यः पिप्पलम् स्वाद्वत्ति, अनशन्नन्यो अभिचाकशीति॥ (Mundaka Upanishat)

Two birds with brilliant wings are sitting friendly on the same tree. One eats and enjoys the sweet leaves of the Pippala tree, while the other observes the eating bird without indulging itself in eating. Here the body is picturized as a tree. The two birds correspond to one Jeeva and the other paramaatma. They are sitting friendly on the same tree or in the same body. Among them, Jeeva enjoys the fruits of his actions without thinking of the others. The other one, Paramatma, is silently observing Jeeva enjoying the fruits.

Thus paramatma remains only as a sakshi (witness) when Jeevatma experiencing the results of his own willful actions.

ఇరువదినాల్గు తత్త్వముల నేర్పడి
ప్రాకృతమైన దేహమే
తరువట, పైడి రెక్కల పతంగము
లచ్చట రెండు జీవు(డి

శ్వరు(డని; యందు కర్మ ఫల
చర్వణ చేసెడి పక్షి జీవు(డే
పొరి పొరి(బుట్టు, వేరొక(డు
పొంపిరి పోవును సాక్షిభూతు(డై. (My Yatirajiyamu)

For the one following the obligatory duties prescribed by the Vedas, without longing for the fruits of the actions, but only performing them to please the Lord, and praying the Lord to release him from the clutches of this life and death cycle of Samsara and surrendering himself completely to Him as the only solace, the Lord, out of compassion, will send him to a proper teacher to help him evolve further.

'panith thalai veezha' – Just as for the one who is in the scorching sun, a cold shower will be very relieving, in the same way, the one who is looking for a way out from this life after life suffering, the compassionate grace of the teacher will be a great blessing. Their life will be blessed. When the Gopikas perform the ritual following the rules laid down by the priests, with complete devotion, they will be blessed both by priests and the Lord. 'then ilangaik komaanaich chetra' - When Ravana was occupying other kingdoms and kidnapping the wives of others, hurting others devotes and sages, Lord took the form of Shree Ramachandra to kill him.

The desires to steal others' property and kidnap the wives of others to enjoy, hurt innocent people, etc., are adharmic and arise in mind engulfed in bad qualities involving kaama, krodha, etc. These are considered the six inner enemies more dangerous than any external enemies. One can fight with the enemies outside, but it is impossible to get rid of these inner enemies by self-effort. These six inner enemies are kaama (desire for sense objects), krodha (anger when one does not get what is desired), lobha (greed), moha (delusion), mada (arrogance), matsaram (jealousy). However much one tries to get rid of them, they keep sprouting like the heads of Ravana.

The only way to get rid of them is by associating with the noble people (sat sangha), following the teachings of the great masters, eating sattvic food, devotional prayers to the Lord, etc. These will slowly get rid of six enemies that arose due to Rajo guna. When these are gone, the mind becomes serene, and one can perform the service of the Lord without any interruptions. That service alone will save the Jeeva and help him in his salvation.

Some teach that Jnaanam alone will lead to one's liberation. ज्ञानविहिनः सर्वमतेन, मुक्तिं न भजति जन्मशतेन॥ (Bhajagovindam) without jnaanam or the knowledge of the absolute, one cannot think of liberation even in hundreds of births. Thus some claim that Jnaanam alone will lead to liberation, and quote ज्ञानादेव तु कैवल्यम् only jnana will lead one to salvation. On the other hand, Lord Krishna taught in Geeta, Jnaana, Bhakti, and Karma yogas, saying that any one of the three will lead the seeker to liberation.

The forest woman, Shabari, and the bird, Jatayu, gained liberation. Is it by jnaanam? If this rule is applied, then, even of the thousands who with the knowledge of 'अथातो धर्मजिज्ञासा', thereby gaining the knowledge of all Vedas, and performing the assigned karmas as prescribed by Vedas and gaining the knowledge of Brahman, will not be getting any liberation. Then what about the fate of simple devotees of the Lord? Is that what the teacher of Geeta taught? It sounds ridiculous.

ఏ వేదంబు పఠించె లూత? భుజగం
  బే శాస్త్రముల్ చూచె? దా
నే విద్యాభ్యసనం బొనర్చె(గరి?
  చెంచేమంత్ర మూహించె? టో
ధావిర్భావ నిదానముల్
  చదువులయ్యా? గావు, నీ పాదసం
సేవాసక్తియ గాక జంతు
  తతికిన్ శ్రీకాళహస్తీశ్వరా? (Dhurjati)

Thus, serving the Lord with complete devotion is the only means for Jeevas for their liberation.

The endless cycle of birth and death for Jeeves results from their selfish actions. Only to experience the result of their past actions, they are taking birth to suitable life forms. At last, by their good deeds, they have gained life in human form, where they can act intelligently. Out of extreme compassion, Lord Krishna taught humanity the paths for their liberation from this endless cycle. These paths are called yogas, as in karma yoga, etc. The Lord called them dharmas.

This universe is due to maayaa, which is Bhagavan's shakti or force. Only those who live dharmic life, thus pleasing only the Lord, can cross this ocean of Maaya. Hence Krishna says, 'माम् एवये प्रपद्यंते मायाम् एताम् तरंति ते' (Geeta 7:14). By saying माम् एवये – only by surrendering to Me, one can cross this maaya of Mine. Hence, service to other Gods will gain the world benefits but not Moksha.

ఇతరుగాక నిర్ఝర సురేశ
    గిరీశ సరస్వతీశ్వరుల్
తత్తడి(బుత్తడిన్ సుతుల దారల
    భూముల వాహ గేహ సం
పత్తుల నిందిరాపతి కృపా
    ప్రతిపాదిత శక్తి(గాని, కిం
చిత్తది యంతవత్తు, పరిశీలన
    చేసిన శాశ్వతమ్ము కో? (My Yatirajiyamu)

Stop becoming devotees of other Gods and give up chanting the names of other gods for mantra, and all other pursuits for liberation other than complete surrender to the Lord Narayana, remembering the Lord's assurance as His final teaching in Geeta, as सर्वधर्मान् परित्यज्य ... if one prays as He is the only solace, Lord will remove all his sins and give him the moksha. That is His promise.

Most Human beings spend their precious time enjoying sense-pleasures. Only one in hundreds or even one in cores, will be really interested in solvation. Krishna gives statistics in the sloka, मनुष्यानाम् सहस्रेषु कस्चित् यतति सिद्धये ..of the thousands of people very few even think of liberation. Very few of those who think of it try towards that. How many seekers can declare, 'Lord is calling me to come to moksha, and I have to renounce house, wife, property, etc.,' and be ready to go immediately?' बहूनाम् जन्मनामंते ज्ञानवान्' after taking many births, due to many merits earned several births, one gets a desire for liberation from this cycle of birth and death.

One who does not have any desire for sense-enjoyments, even rushee like Shree Yamana, etc., when he was told that 'Shree Ranganatha is ready to give you moksha, please start immediately' apparently responded by saying, please give me two more days I will pack and come. If that is the case of a person who does not have any desire for sense-enjoyments, what to talk about those who are fully engrossed in the sense-pleasures?

Goda Devi says the gopies, longing to serve the Lord, giving up everything, *'manaththhukku iniyaanaip paadavum'* are singing the glories of the Lord.

Like that, we all must be ready to serve the Lord and sing His glories; instead of denying the company of devotees, you have closed the door and still sleeping. Without getting up early in the morning, wasting god-given precious human life by indulging in sense-pleasures is like 'asking useless charcoal from the divine tree (kalpataruvu), which is capable of giving anything the devotees ask.

Pasuram:

ఆ(కొన్న లేగల నాదరమ్ముగన(బిల్చి
   ఎనుములు తచ్చింత మనము గరిగి
పాల్ చేపి చన్నుల(టడి జాలువారి యి
   ల్లెల్ల జంటాలమై యుల్ల సిల్లు
ధన్యురాలా! మంచు తలలపై గురియంగ(
   దడియుచు నీ యింటి గడపపట్టి
సీతను చెరగొన్న యాతుధానుని లంక
   నేతను కాలుని వాత(ద్రోసి
సాధుమానస మానంద జలధిదేల్చి
నట్టి శ్రీరామచంద్రు నోరార(టాడి
నప్పటికి మారుమాటాడ, వందరెరిగి
నార లింకేని లెమ్మ టంగారుబొమ్మ.

PASURAM 13

Introduction:

Goda Devi is trying to wake up another girl.

புள்ளின் வாய் கீண்டானைப் பொல்லா அரக்கனைக்
    கிள்ளிக் களைந்தானைக் கீர்த்திமை பாடிப்போய்
பிள்ளைகள் எல்லாரும் பாவைக் களம் புக்கார்
    வெள்ளி எழுந்து வியாழம் உறங்கிற்று
புள்ளும் சிலம்பின காண்! போது அரிக்கண்ணினாய்
    குள்ளக் குளிரக் குடைந்து நீராடாதே
பள்ளிக் கிடத்தியோ பாவாய்! நீ நன்னாளால்
    கள்ளம் தவிர்த்து கலந்து ஏல் ஓர் எம்பாவாய்

Pullin vaay keendaanaip pollaa arakkanaik

Killik kalaindhaanaik keerththi mai paadip poyp

Pillaigal ellaarum paavaik kalambukkaar

Velli ezhundhu viyaazham urangitru

Pullum silambina kaan podharik kanninaay

Kullak kulirak kudaindhu neeraadaadhae

Pallik kidaththiyo! Paavaay! Nee nan naalaal

Kallam thavirndhu kalandhaelor embaavaay (13)

Meaning: *'podharik kanninaay'*, Oh! Lady, your beauty is pouring out through your eyes which look like fully blossomed flowers. The more we see, the more we feel like seeing them. If we are feeling like this, what about the dark, beautiful-skinned Krishna when He sees your eyes? After gagging into your eyes, He may not want to see any other lady's eyes. When you have such beautiful eyes, is it fair to close them and sleep? Is it fair? At least, for once, open your eyes and see. 'velliezhundhuviyaazhamurangit ru', morning has come, and the Guru (the planet/star) has set already. Moon is gone. Can't you see? Would you not Him see any other eyes? When you have such beautiful eyes, how come you close them and sleep? Is it fair? At least open your eyes and see. 'velli ezhundhu viyaazham urangitru', morning has come, and the moon is gone. Can't you see?

You may not know since you have closed your eyes. 'Pullum silambina kaan' the birds got up and made noise. Could you not hear those sounds? Do your ears also have lids to close them, making you not hear?

'ఏకాంతమున భగవద్ధ్యానుసంధానమునునున్న నాకు బాహ్యప్రపంచము తెలియలే దందువేమొ', Are you saying that you are deeply meditating on the Lord and therefore unaware of the external world? If so, it is OK. If worldly affairs like 'morning has come, the birds are already making noise, etc.' are not entering your brain, you should at least listen to the Lord's glories and songs that we all like to hear.

'pullin vaay keendaanaip pollaa arakkanaik killik kalaindhaanaik keerththi mai paadip' All our friends are passing through these streets singing Krishna's episodes about how he killed all demons/rakshasas, helped Bheema (also known as Vrukodara, the second among the Pandavas) to fight, and how he killed Bakasura. They are also singing the glories of Shree Ramachandra, who chopped off the head of Ravana, who has done terrible demonic actions like kidnapping the wives of others. All our friends, singing these glories of the Lord, went through these streets. At least have those songs not reached your ears?

Opening your eyes and find out if they were here, calling you so many times to wake you up. Since you are pretending to sleep, they got tired and left. But we stayed back to make sure you got up, and while waiting for you in the process, we got delayed. At least now you get up. It is still not too late. We can rush and join them. With the commitment to do the Margasira ritual, we first purify ourselves in the flowing cold waters of the river. Now, stop pretending to sleep, get up, complete your prayers at the altar, and join us soon. When we have the opportunity to pray, 'nan naalaal', during this holy time to be with Lord Krishna and offer our prayers to Him, why waste our time with minds dwelling in imaginary worlds by laying down on the bed? To be able to receive the blessings of Lord Krishna, let us purify our bodies by taking a bath in the cold waters of the river early in the morning. If we delay, the ladies who just now left after waiting for you for a long time will complete the ritual on time and receive the blessings of the Lord. Hence, get up quickly and let us go and join them.

When we are doing good things, we should do them as quickly as possible. There are sayings, शुभस्य शीग्रम्, for good things faster the better, and आलस्यम् अमृतम् विषम्, when you delay even the nectar becomes a poison.

Pasuram:

పులుగులు రోదసేసె(టొడిచెను చుక్కయు
            గురు(డస్తమించెను కువలయాక్షి,
పులు(గు(జీల్చినవాని(, టొలసుదిండిని సంహా
            రించినవాని(గీర్తించుకొనుచు
సఖియలెల్లరు మున్న చని చేరి కొన్నారు
            భామినీమణి నేము పట్టునకును
ఈ మేలిదినమున నిందా(క లేవక
            పడకను వీడక పవ్వళించి
పొరలు చున్నావదేమిటే? పూవుటోణి!
కపట నిద్దుర విడనాడి, కలసి మెలసి
యువతళించెను జలముల నిందువదన
మునిగి నీరాడుదము రమ్ము మోహనాంగి.

PASURAM 14

Introduction:

Goda Devi is trying to wake up another girl who is still sleeping.

உங்கள் புழக்கடைத் தோட்டத்து வாவியுள்
   செங்கழு நீர் வாய் நெகிழ்ந்து ஆம்பல் வாய் கூம்பின
   காண்
செங்கல் பொடிக் கூறை வெண்பல் தவத்தவர்
   தங்கள் திருக்கொயில் சங்கிடுவான் போகின்றார்
எங்களை முன்னம் எழுப்புவான் வாய் பேசும்
   நங்காய் எழுந்திராய் நாணாதாய் நாவுடையாய்
சங்கொடு சக்கரம் ஏந்தும் தடக்கையன்
   பங்கயக் கண்ணானைப் பாடு ஏல் ஓர் எம்பாவாய்

Ungal puzhakkadaith thottaththu vaaviyul

Sengazhuneer vaay negizhndhu aambal vaay koombina kaan

Sengar podik koorai venbal thavaththavar

Thangal thirukkoyil sangiduvaan podhanraar

Engalai munnam ezhuppuvaan vaaypaesum

Nangaay ezhundhiraay naanaadhaay naavudaiyaay

Sangodu chakkaram aendhum thadakkaiyan

Pangayak kannaanaip paadaelor embaavaay (14)

Meaning: Oh! A gem among ladies! What a naughty person you are! You said you would get up early and then go around and wake all of us. You are not getting up even after we tried to wake you up! You blame us that we have not gotten up! What a naughty girl you are! Just because you have a tongue to speak does not mean you should say, ' that is not yet morning.' Do you think we are lying? Look outside. Look at the well near you. The lotus flowers are already blooming, seeing the sun and mocking you, seeing your closed eyes. Aren't you a proud girl? Shame on you. Get up quickly. Please open your eyes, which are like thousands of broad leaves. Look around and see how late it is. Your eyes, like black lotuses, have closed themselves, as though out of jealousy, after looking at other colorful lotuses that are fully blooming. At least they should tell you that it is already morning.

You may say, 'who is going to go near the well and examine it.' It is OK. At least open your doors and see the streets outside.

Open your eyes and see three sages of the mutt (jeers) moving from one temple to the other. It seems they have collected all the longing desires for the objects in their minds. By throwing all that junk out, they look very serene and sattvik. They are wearing orange robes symbolizing the fire of knowledge. They look very divine because of the blessings they receive by worshiping the Lord daily. They are also moving around, blessing other devotees who are serving the Lord in the temple. You can look at them. At least open your eyes and see how many devotes are moving around in and out of the temple.

Explanation:

Both lotuses and lilies have a short life. As though they are teaching us that life is very short and any apparent glory is only short-lived. The water lilies were blooming the whole night and are now fading away in the morning. On the other hand, while closing their petals in the night, the lotuses begin to bloom again once morning comes.

The water lilies are teaching us that once we have secured a birth in this human form, during our short life, we should not be going for external material things and temporary sense pleasures. Instead, we should strive for eternal, everlasting happiness that we can secure with the grace of God. Hence, all the time, we should go after entities that do not lose their values in time, such as the Lord who has eternal glories, 'pangayak kannaanaip', Pundarikaksha, the one whose eyes are similar to the shape of the petals of the lotus flower. If we serve Him with no other diversion and surrender completely to Him, He will protect us. 'sangodu chakkaram aendhum thadakkaiyan'. In his right hand, He is wearing the disk that can destroy the enemies in His right hand. For Jeevas, the enemies are the ones who obstruct them from getting what is best for them. These inner enemies are kama (desire), krodha (anger), lobha (greed), mada (arrogance), moha (delusion), matsarya (jealousy), sanchita and aagaami karmas. Lord can destroy these using his disk. Hence

He is called 'chakraayudha'; one always wears the disk to destroy evil.

The things that prevent us from securing permanent, eternal happiness are our attachments to our bodies and the feeling that we are independent conscious entities. In addition, some also have 'अहम् ब्रह्मास्मि' 'I am Brahman,' a misconceived understanding. In addition, they try to preach their misunderstanding to others. The only one who can remove these misconceptions to the roots is the one who is carrying the invincible disk in His right hand. The Lord is praised compared to Jevas as highly versatile, with long hands, fully decorated, and divine personality.

In the 11th Chapter of Geeta, He is described as Virat Purusha – with thousands of heads and hands, etc. Even Arjuna got frightened looking at the Virat Purusha. Hence for us, He is visualized with His divine form with four hands, wearing a conch and disk in his two hands and pleasing looks. Instead of the frightening Virat form with fierce sun and moon as His two eyes, we like *pangayak kannaanaip*, only the lotus-eyed one with a pleasing personality and who stole our hearts. Hence after seeing the frightening Virat form, Arjuna prays to see Lord in His pleasing form.

अदृष्टपूर्वम् हृषितोऽस्मिदृष्ट्वा भयेन च प्रव्यथितम् मनो मे|

तदेव मे दर्शय देवरूपम् प्रसीद देवेश जगन्निवास||
(Geeta 11:45)

Oh! Lord! I am excited to see a wonderful form I have never seen before. At the same time, my mind is filled with fear. Oh! Lord! Please bless me by showing your familiar, pleasing form.

किरीटिनम् गदिनम् चक्रहस्तम् इच्छामि त्वाम्
द्रष्टुमहम् तथैव।
तेनैव रूपेण चतुर्भुजेन सहस्रबाहो भव विश्वमूर्ते।
(Geeta 11:46)

Oh! I desire to see your pleasing form again with your four hands, carrying the disk, conch, and mace.

Hence, we too, desire to see His pleasing glorious happy form and offer prayers with complete devotion to serving Him in that form. We will be blessed with eternal happiness. Hence Goda Devi says, Oh! Girl! Please get up quickly and come and join us for the ritual.

The statement, 'in the middle of the well, the lotuses are blooming while the water lilies look faded,' has a deeper philosophical meaning. The body is like a well. In that, the lilies that were blooming before and now getting faded indicate that the Jeevas experiencing the results of their actions that give happiness and sorrow. In the same well, the blooming lotus indicates Paramatma. There are no fruits of action for Paramatma. He remains as a Sakshi or witness – thus indicating the Mundaka Upanishad sloka,

द्वा सुपर्णा सयुजा सखाया समानं वृक्षं परिषस्वजाते।
तयोरन्यः पिप्पलं स्वाद्वत्त्यनश्नन्नन्य
अभिचाकशीति ॥ (Mundaka Upanishat)

On the same tree, there are two birds with golden wings; one is eating the fruits (of action) while the other is just observing the previous bird eating. In the same way, the faded lilies are like Jeevas, experiencing the fruits of their actions, while the blooming lotus is like Paramatma inside the body. Jeevas, even though close to the Lord, are still suffering as they are bound by the Prakruti (maayaa).

By serving the 'thavaththavar' the noble Acharyas, the Jeevas get blessed. These noble Acharyas, *sengar podik koorai venbal*, are wearing orange robes. Orange color stands for attachments – attachments for worldly possessions and the desire to enjoy them. These were thrown out from their bodies and now exist only as the outer dress. When the desires are gone, then the anger is also not there – कामात् क्रोधोभिजायते ... प्रणश्यति -says Geeta. When rajo and tamo gunas are removed from the mind, only sattva guna will bloom, and as a result, good qualities like shanti (peace), sama (mind control), dama (sense control), uparati(absence of desires for worldly pleasures) titiksha (forbearance) will develop.

We need to approach such Acharyas and get guidance from them for our own spiritual growth. To those who approach such Acaryas, 'thangal thirukkoyil', they will instruct the disciples on the means to reach the highest goal in life, the abode of Shreeman Narayana. They will pass on the key, 'shang' , in the form of the ashtottara mantra (eight-lettered mantra), with the help of which one can enter the abode of Lord Narayana. Those who recite the ashtottara mantra japa with full devotion to the Lord *sangodu chakkaram aendhum thadakkaiyan*, He will destroy the very disturbing six inner enemies – kaama, etc., that are obstructing the progress of His devotees using His powerful disk and install in them with sama, etc., six great qualities by using His sacred conch. The Lord will look after their yoga and kshema, all their needs, to ensure their progress. Unlike going after temporary glory like water lilies, like lotuses, seeking permanent, eternal happiness in the abode of 'pangayak kannaanaip', the one with lotus eyes, Lord Narayana. For such devotees, the Lord will bless them with unending, eternal happiness. Hence one should approach proper Acharyas, receive the ashtottara mantra, do the Japa with utmost reverence, and surrender completely at the feet of the Lord (sharanaagati) to secure the permanent release from this cycle of birth and death and reach the highest abode of Shreeman Narayana. That is the highest goal in life for all beings.

Pasuram:

పూ(దో(ట నడబావి(టూచె కెందామరలు
కాంచుమా ముకుళించె కలువపూలు
కావు లీనుమడుంగు కటి జుట్టి, తెల్లని
పలుచాలు తోడి తపస్వివరులు

దేవాలయము తల్పు(దీయ (గుంచిక (టూని
        వెడలుచున్నారమ్మ పడ(తిమిన్న
'మిమ్ము ముందుగ వచ్చి మేలుకొల్పెద' నంచు
        మాటిచ్చి లేపని మాటకారి
దాన, యికనైన లెమ్ము మందాక్షిహీన,
పంకరుహనేత్రు వ్యాదీర్ఘ బాహువులను
దర్శనము పాంచజన్యము(దాల్చువాని
కీర్తనము సేయ రావమ్మ కీరవాణి|

PASURAM 15

Goda Devi wakes up another girl who is deeply immersed in singing the glories of Lord Krishna and does not get up for the ritual. This pasuram is in the conversational style.

எல்லே! இளங்கிளியே இன்னம் உறங்குதியோ
   சில்லென்று அழையேன் மின் நங்கைமீர்
   போதருகின்றேன்
வல்லை உன் கட்டுரைகள் பண்டே உன் வாய் அறிதும்
   வல்லீர்கள் நீங்களே நான் தான் ஆயிடுக
ஒல்லை நீ போதாய் உனக்கு என்ன வேறு உடையை
   எல்லாரும் போந்தாரோ? போந்தார் போந்து
   எண்ணிக் கொள்
வல்லானை கொன்றானை மாற்றாரை மாற்று அழிக்க
   வல்லானை மாயானை பாடு ஏல் ஓர் எம்பாவாய்

Ellae! Ilam kiliyae innam urangudhiyo

Chil enru azhaiyaen min nangaiyeer podharuginraen

Vallai un katturaigal pandae un vaay aridhum

Valleergal neengalae naanae thaan aayiduga

Ollai nee podhaay unakkenna vaerudaiyai

Ellaarum pondhaaro pondhaar pondhu ennikkol

Vallaanai konraanai maatraarai maatrazhikka-

Vallaanai maayanaip paadaelor embaavaay (15)

Meaning: This is the last pasuram that involves Goda Devi trying to wake up girls to join her in performing the Margasira ritual. It contains some summary statements used in the previous nine pasurams that involve waking up the sleeping girls. It is in conversation style.

They: Oh! Girl! You are not getting up even now. You said before that you would get up first and wake up all of us. Yet, you are still sleeping. You made all boasting statements before that we should all get up early and do perform the Margasira ritual beautifully in a big way. And you are still sleeping and not getting up. Please open the doors for us; we have been calling you all the time. You just talked like a parrot which does not mean what it says. *keeravaaNii*, Oh! Boasting girl! It is alright. At least get-up and join us immediately, as we are in a hurry. To these calling people, the girl responds

She: Do not shout unnecessarily. Also, do not find fault with me. I am coming just now.

They: What a cunning lady you are! We are not surprised by your response as you have done this before.

She: You are the ones who are cunning. Alright, let me assume that I am at fault for your sake. Now, what do you want me to do?

They: What is there to say? You are enjoying yourself thinking of the Lord; in the process, you have forgotten to get up on time. Is it not more joyful to revel in the Lord together than all by yourself? Come, join us, and we will all pray together to the one who has subdued the elephant,

Kuralayapidam, and fought and killed the Mustikaasura and Banaasuras, the one who is the master of maayaa and now in the very pleasing idol form.

She: I am coming now. Am I the only one who was late? Did all others come and join?

They: You are just wasting time and just talking to escape the blame. Yet not getting up from the bed? Who is stopping you from coming? What a selfish girl you are! We already said that we all came and waiting for you. You are still sleeping on the bed and asking us silly questions. If you do not believe what we are saying, you must come and count to see if all have come or not.

Explanation: When people of a similar background are together and share their enjoyment with others, their happiness is much more than each one enjoying separately. एक स्वादु न भुंजीत, even if it is a small amount, it is better to share with others than enjoy oneself. In addition, there is no better happiness than the happiness one gets in singing the glories of the Lord, remembering Him all the time, and contemplating and meditating on Him.

అంబుజోదర దివ్య పాదారవింద
చింతనామృతపాన విశేషమత్త
చిత్తమేరీతి నితరంటు(జేరనేర్చు?
వినుత గుణశీల మాటలు వేయు నేల. (Potana)
అమృతరసమొలుక నీదు పాదారవింద
మందు మది చేర్చి యెవ్వ డన్యంటు గోరు
తుమ్మెద మరంద తుందిలతోయజాత
ముండ నుమ్మెత్త(జూచనే యూరకైన|

This is the essence of the Pasuram.

Pasuram:

ఏందాక నిద్రింతువే? లేతకిరమా!
   వరవర్ణినులు మీరు దురుసు పల్కు
లాడ(టోకుం డిదే యరుగు దెంచితి నేను,
   గట్టిదానవు, నీదు గడుసుమాట
లన్నిన్ను మే మెల్ల మున్నె యెఱుంగుదు
   మతివ, మీరల దిట్ట నగుదుగాక
నేన? యేమందురు? నీవొక్కతే వేఱ
   భోగసౌభాగ్యమ్ము వొందనేల?
అరుగుదేరుము వేగిర, మందరరుగు
దెంచిరే? వచ్చి రేతెంచి యెంచికొనుము
మత్త మాతంగ సంహర్త మాయలాని
రమ్ము గీర్తింప దుర్దమారాతిఘూతి.

PASURAM 16

Introduction:

After waking up all the girls who are interested in joining the ritual, they all go to the town where Lord Krishna lives and request the gatekeeper to let them in to worship the Lord.

நாயகனாய் நின்ற நந்த கோபனுடைய
    கோயில் காப்பானே! கொடித் தோன்றும் தோரண
வாயில் காப்பானே! மணிக்கதவம் தாள் திறவாய்
    ஆயர் சிறுமியரோமுக்கு, அறைபறை
மாயன் மணி வண்ணன் நென்னலே வாய் நேர்ந்தான்
    தூயோமாய் வந்தோம் துயில் எழப் பாடுவான்
வாயால் முன்னம் முன்னம் மாற்றாதே அம்மா நீ
    நேய நிலைக் கதவம் நீக்கு ஏல் ஓர் எம்பாவாய்

Naayaganaay ninra nandhagopan udaiya

Koyil kaappaanae! Kodi thonrum thorana-

Vaayil kaappaanae! Manik kadhavam thaal thiravaay

Aayar sirumiyaromukku arai parai-

Maayan mani vannan nennalae vaay naerndhaan

Thooyomaay vandhom thuyil ezhap paaduvaan

Vaayaal munnam munnam maatraadhae ammaa! Nee-

Naeya nilaik kadhavam neekkaelor embaavaay (16)

Meaning: Nanda baba is the leader of all local cowherd leaders. He is the head of that community. In contrast to the houses of citizens, his house is distinct and majestic. The town is enormous. For that town, there is a fort protecting the town. Immediately inside the fort is a big, majestic pillar and decorated big entrance to the town. If one goes further inside, there is a big building with many sections. There are many rooms used for different purposes, including the entrance hall where guests are entertained, bathrooms, dining halls, bedrooms, etc. Near the fort entrance, gatekeepers are protecting the entrance.

To overcome the lack of good rains and drought, the cowherd elders of the town asked the cowherd girls to organize the prayer ritual under the leadership of Lord Krishna. Interestingly, the elders who had prevented the association of the young girls with Lord Krishna now asked them to do the ritual under his leadership. The young girls, who love to be with Krishna, are very much excited to do this ritual. They all got up early, joined together, and went to Krishna's house to wake him up. However, at the very entrance, the gatekeepers stopped them from entering the building.

Nanda's place was not that restricted before. However, the security was increased because of too many attacks by demons like Putana, etc. The demons were coming in various disguised forms, in the form of ladies or gents, animal forms like horses, or even inert-looking objects like cartwheels, etc. They were coming in various forms and shapes to hurt the little Krishna. Hence Nanda initiated strict entrance rules and screened the visitors.

Hence the security at the entrance is meticulous, particularly for the visitors coming very early in the morning, mainly when the light is not sufficient to screen thoroughly. Hence the entrance to the temple of the Lord is difficult.

Hence the guards were ready to question the young girls who were trying to enter about their details, who they were, and the purpose of their visit that early in the morning. Hence anticipating the problem, the girls addressed the guards as *'koyil kaappaanae!'* Oh! Guards to this Temple!

Krishana spends a lot of time outside the residence and moves freely with the local citizens of that village, 'golla palle'. The population is limited. The guards, whenever they were outside the palace gates, watched the activities of the public on the streets and recognized the girls. These girls used to play freely with Lord Krishna, singing and dancing everywhere in the village, streets, parks, banks of the Yamuna river, mountains and trees, fields where the cows graze, etc. Hence, the guards let the girls go inside without stopping them, considering them their people.

After the fort entrance, there is the great pillar. Once that is crossed, there is the big entrance where the diamond-studded heavy doors are present, and the doors are locked. The key of the locks is hanging near the waist of the big guard. For him, these girls are not that familiar.

The girls felt he might not allow them to go inside as easily as the fort guards did. Hence they started requesting him to let them inside.

'*kodi thonrum thorana vaayil kaappaanae! Manik kadhavam thaal thiravaay*', Sir, please remove the locks of this temple entrance and allow us to go inside. Just unlocking will not help since we are girls who cannot push open these heavy doors, which are very strong. The two doors are joined together, and difficult for us to separate them. Hence, *naeya nilaik kadhavam neekkaelor*'- please push open the doors for us.

'If you say that you do not know who we are and cannot let new people in,' please do not say that. We are not strangers. We are girls from this golla palle only. We are very simple people without any ulterior motives. We have played with Krishna before. Yesterday only Krishna told us to come early in the morning. We are asked to do the ritual by the elders of the village. Krishna said he would give us the tools we needed to do the ritual. He does not go back on his words.

We have to sing Suprabhatam to Lord Krishna and wake him up. For that reason, we have come here with pure hearts after purifying ourselves in the river. If you do not let us enter quickly and we are late, you and we will be blamed. Hence please let us enter the temple without obstructing us and causing further delay in performing the ritual.

Implied meaning:

Devotees should go near God only after receiving a blessing from Acharya. In addition, when we go to the temple, we have to project a devotional attitude in terms of dress, speech, and mental attitude – manasaa-vaachaa-karmanaa. Lord recognizes the attitude with which the devotee is approaching Him. The dress and the speech should reflect the attitude of service and surrender to Lord Vishnu. The poem below shows how.

ये कंठलग्नतुलसीनलिनाक्षमाला येबाहुमूलपरिचिहिनत शंखचक्राः

ये वा ललाटफलके लसनदूर्ध्वपुंड्राः ते वैष्णवाः भुवन माशु पवित्रयन्ति॥

Surrendering to the Lord Vishnu becomes evident with twelve Vaishnava decorative marks on the forehead and the upper body, the Lord's symbols of shanku (conch) and chakra (disk) done on the shoulders (this is done during the purification function called samaasrayanam), the proper upper cloth sheet covering the body, for both women and men, Vaishnava marks on the forehead, etc. They should be chanting the Lakshmi Narayana sacred chanting or stotras.

These are the external indicators only that others can see. However, Lord mainly sees the inner purity of the mind. The mind should not have jealousy for others but tend to forgive others" faults, friendliness to all, expression of joy while seeing the prosperity of others, conversation with a smile, desire to see the best in others, control of senses, and dispassion towards the sense-pleasures, tolerance to others faults, ready to help others, gratitude for what was given, etc. They show the purity of the mind.

'thooyomaay vandhom' thus having purified externally, with the guards' blessings, the girls entered the temple. In the same way, with the blessings of the Acharya and purified mind, one can enter into His sanctum Santorum.

To fulfill the desires for the liberation of such devotees, the Lord, *'vannan nennalae vaay naerndhaan'* has already promised before. He gave His word, 'if you serve me with pure minds with an attitude of complete surrender, I will fulfill any desire of yours.' If we do our part, He promised to bless us without paying attention to other factors such as *'Jaati, kula, linga'*, our caste, man or woman, etc.

रामो द्विर्नाभिभाषते – Rama does not have a double tongue, saying one thing here and another thing there. Even when he is going to face extreme hardship in the forest, he fulfilled his father's promise and went to the forest for 14 years. Now as the Lord, does He violate His promise now.

ఇంతి పుమాంసుడంచు, మది

వృద్ధు(డు బాలు(డనంచు, మర్త్యు(డన్

జంతువునంచు, లెక్కిడక సర్వ

లకే నభయంబు నిత్తు నా

వంతది "సర్వదా శరణ

వర్ణితు(డన్ నను గావు" మంట నీ

వంతని యుంట నీ యెదుట
వాంఛ వచించితి చెన్నకేశవా| (My Keshavaprapatti)

Pasuram:

మహనీయ! నందుని మాళిగ కాపరీ!
ధ్వజపటాలంకృత ద్వారపాల
గొల్లపిల్లలము, గైకొనుము వందనము, ర
త్న ఖచిత ద్వారటంధనము తెరువు
మణివర్ణు(డౌ మాయి మాట యిచ్చెను నిన్న
మాకు డక్కియొసంగ మాన్యచరిత
పరిశుద్ధతరలమై యరుగుదెంచితి మయ్య
నిద్దుర లేపను నీలవర్ణు
తొట్టతొలుతనె మము నడ్డుపెట్టు మాట
లాడటోకము, కదిసిన యరరములను
నీవ నీచేత విఘటించి, పోవనిమ్ము
మమ్ము లోనికి సుప్రభాతమ్ము(టాడ.

PASURAM 17

Introduction:

The Gopika girls went inside to wake up Nanda and others.

Pasuram:

அம்பரமே தண்ணீரே சோறே அறஞ்செய்யும்
    எம்பெருமான் நந்தகோபாலா எழுந்திராய்
கொம்பனார்க்கு எல்லாம் கொழுந்தே குல விளக்கே
    எம்பெருமாட்டி யசோதாய் அறிவுறாய்
அம்பரம் ஊடு அறுத்து ஓங்கி உலகளந்த
    உம்பர் கோமானே! உறங்காது எழுந்திராய்
செம்பொற் கழலடிச் செல்வா பலதேவா
    உம்பியும் நீயும் உறங்கேல் ஓர் எம்பாவாய்

Ambaramae thanneerae sorae aram seyyum

Emberumaan nandhagopaalaa ezhundhiraay

Kombanaarkku ellaam kozhundhae kula vilakkae

Emberumaatti yasodhaay arivuraay

Ambaram ooda aruththu Ongi ulagu alandha

Umbar komaanae urangaadhu ezhundhiraay

Sem por kazhaladich chelvaa baladhaevaa

Umbiyum neeyun urangaelor embaavaay (17)

Meaning: The girls who have entered Nada's palace are waking up the people inside. First, they wake up Nanda, the head of the household. He is a noble person who donates clothes to wear and food to eat to those in need. The noble people establish tents that give pure and cold drinking water to those who are very thirsty, particularly in summer. For those who were hungry, they established feeding houses. Food and drinks are essential things for survival.

If we donate uncooked food materials, they can be misused. But the cooked food and the drinks cannot be misused. None can eat more than he can. The cooked food cannot be stored for days ahead, particularly in summer. After eating cooked rice, even if you throw the excess, other living beings eat that and survive. If we give wealth, the receiver does not say I am contented with what I have received, whereas cooked food is different, as he cannot eat more than what his stomach can take. Nanda is of the type who donates food and drinks for the needy.

Unlike other living beings, wearing a dress is essential for human beings to protect their dignity. Sometimes it is even more important than even food. People can live without food for some time but not without dress. Nanda donates a lot of clothes for those who need them.

The Gopika girls started saying, 'Oh! Great soul! Nanda Gopala! Please wake up. It is said that even Gods like to hear people praising them. Hence Vedas starts first praising the Gods.

To get work done, we have to praise the people in charge. The person may be very hard to deal with, but he will become soft once we start praising him. It is well known that Nanda loves his son, Krishna, very much. He would not tolerate disturbing his son. Fearing that some demon or rakshasa can come in some form and cause problems to Krishna, Nanda made his son sleep next to him. Hence, the Gopika girls thought that if we woke up Krishna first, Nanda might get up. He will be angry with us, thinking that we have disturbed Krishna. He may drive us out. Hence they try to wake up Nanda first.

'nandhagopaalaa ezhundhiraay', saying that if we wake him up, he may ignore us. But if we praise him a little bit, he will be soft and would hesitate to dismiss our subsequent requests. Hence, they called him! Oh! Noble, generous soul! You provide the basic necessities for surviving: food, drink, and clothes for the poor. You, who are so generous even to unknown people, please grant us our request since you know us very well. You are a Gopala, and we are Gopika girls. We came here for some purpose; please grant us our wish.

Viswamitra requested for Rama. First, Dasharatha, out of his over-affection for his son, refused to send Rama with Viswamitra. Afterwards, due to the encouragement from Kausalya Devi, He agreed to send Rama. Ladies are inherently more kind. When the Gopika girls could not hear any response from Nanda, they tried to wake up Yasoda Devi next.

'kombanaarkku ellaam kozhundhae kula vilakkae emberumaatti yasodhaay arivuraay' Amma! Yasoda Devi! At least you wake up Shree Krishna. You are a shining light for the whole cowherd families. Not just light, You gave us the embodiment of knowledge and happiness, Lord Krishna, who can pass on that knowledge and happiness to all of us. Krishna maybe your son, but He is Paramatma born to uplift not only you but the whole world. He belongs to all of us. Being very generous, it is not fair for you to have Him exclusively for yourself. You need to share Him with everybody. You are 'emberumaatti' our madam, and we are your servants. Who will fulfill our desires other than yourself? Hence Oh! Mother! Please wake up and then wake up our Krishna.

Thus, after waking her up, they started doing suprabhatam to Lord Krishna. 'umbar komaanae urangaadhu ezhundhiraay' Oh! Lord, the master of all Gods! You are the one who is always concerned whether any Rakshaas are trying to harm the Gods, who are your devotees and have completely surrendered to you. The Gods who could not bear the tortures of the Rakshasas, like Hiranya kashipu and Hiranyaksha prayed for you. You did not hesitate to take the birth in the form of Varaha and Narasimha to destroy them. Even though you are a husband of Sree Devi, you made yourself very small as a brahmachari, Vamana, to ask for three small feet of land from Emperor Bali.

You always have an upper hand in giving what the disciples want. देहीति वचनम् कष्टम्, नास्तीति वचनम् ततः', it is very difficult to request someone to give, and similarly difficult to say that I do not have it, when someone asks. But Oh! Lord, you did not feel shy to keep your hand on the receiving end, under the hand of the great emperor. That too, yours is not a small hand. All this drama you played is only to help your disciples who have surrendered to you. Your hand is not ordinary as Potana describes

ఆదిన్ శ్రీసతికొప్పుపై(దనువుపై నంసోత్తరీయంబుపై(
బాదాబ్జంబులపై(గపోలతటిపై(బాలిండ్లపై నూత్నమ
ర్యాదం జెందుకరంటు గ్రిన్దగుట మీ(డై నాకరం టుంట మేల్
గాదే రాజ్యము గిజ్యమున్ సతతమే కాయంటు నాపాయమే.
(Potana)

Keeping your hand down to help your devotees shows your kindness. When you asked Emperor Bali, please give me, he said

వరిచేలంటులో మాడలో ఫలములో
    వన్యంటులో గోవులో
హారులో రత్నములో రథంటులో
    విమ్మృష్టాన్నంటులో కన్యలో
కరులో కాంచనమో నికేతనములో
    గ్రామంటులో భూములో
ధరణీఖండమో కాక యేమడిగెదో
    ధాత్రీ సురేంద్రోత్తమా|

Then when Bali gave you a big list of all things that he can give if you ask, you said

ఒంటివాడ(నాకు నొకటి రెండడుగుల
మేర యిమ్ము , నొమ్మ మేర యొల్ల(
గోర్కెదీర బ్రహ్మకూ(కటి ముట్టెద
దానకుతుకసాంద్ర! దానవేంద్ర!

You asked for only one or two feet of land and nothing else. The King responded to this disguised small boy

ఉన్న మాటలెల్ల నొప్పను విప్రుండ
సత్యగతులు వృద్ధ సమ్మతంబు
లడుగ(దలచి కొంచెమడిగగతివో చెల్ల
దాత పెంపు నొంపు(దలప(వలదె?

As an emperor how can I give such a small one, you responded smiling

గొడుగో జన్నిదమో కమండలువో
నాకున్ ముంజియో దండమో
వడు గే నెక్కడ భూము లెక్కడ
కరుల్ వామాక్షు లశ్వంటు లె
క్కడ నిత్యేచితకర్మ మెక్కడ
మదాకాక్షామింతంటైన మూ(
డడుగుల్ మేరయ త్రోవకిచ్చుటది
బ్రహ్మండంటు నా పాలికిన్|

You insisted Emperor Bali give only three feet of land, claiming that itself is brahmandam for you (you really meant it since you later claimed the brahmandam with your three feet!)

Thus you showed that you would be very satisfied with just three feet of land measured by your tiny feet. Listening to your request, even the Gods got baffled without knowing your ulterior motives. How can they know your Leelas or divine plays?

Only Sukracharya who is well-wisher of his students could suspect your motive. He said,

దనుజేంద్ర! యాతడు ధరణీసురుడు గాడు
దేవకార్యంబు సాధించు కొఱకు
హరి విష్ణు(డవ్యయుం డదితిగర్భంబునన్
గశ్యప సూనుడై కలిగె నకట
యెఱుగ కీతని కోర్కి_ నిచ్చెద నంటివి
దైత్యసంతతి కుపద్రవము వచ్చు
నీ లక్ష్మి(దేజంటు నెలవు నైశ్వర్యంటు
వంచించి యిచ్చు(దా వాసవునకు
మొనసి జగములెల్ల మూ(డుపాదంటుల
నఖిల కాయు(డగుచు నాక్రమించు
సర్వధనము విష్ణుసంసర్జనము సేసి
తడుగు పగిది నెట్టు బ్రదికెదీవు?

He is none other than Lord Vishnu who came here to help the Gods. He is going to make you the poorest of all by taking everything from you. Hence do not give him anything. This is against any dharma. After listening to his teacher Sukracharya, the Emperor did not agree with it and said,

నిరయంటైన నిటంధమైన
ధరణీ నిర్ము, లనంటైన దు

ర్మకరణంటైన(గులాంతమైన
నిజమున రానిమ్మ కానిమ్మ పో
హారు(డైనన్ హరియైన నీరజ
భవుం డభ్యగతుండైన నౌ
దిరుగన్ నేరదు నాదు జిహ్వ
వినుమా ధీవర్య, వేయేటికిన్
మేరువు దలక్రింద్రైనను
బారావారంబు లింక(బాటిన లోలో
ధారుణి రజమై పోయిన(
దారాధ్వము బద్ధమైన(దప్పక యిత్తున్|

Thus, Bali Chakravarti stood on his words, saying that he would never go back on his promise.

To protect the Devas, who are devotees of the Lord, the Lord in the little brahmachari form, Vamana, grew to become so big as to cover with his two feet the entire universe consisting of both lower worlds and upper worlds. He then asked Bali where He should put His third foot. Bali asked Him to place it on his head – thus offering himself entirely to the Lord. That action also blessed Bali, and his grandfather Prahallada was pleased, too, seeing how Bali surrendered himself entirely to the Lord. Lord made Bali the master of the lower worlds, and He stood at his gatekeeper to ensure no disturbing thoughts would enter Bali's mind. In essence, Lord protects whoever surrenders completely.

Hence the Gopika girls say, you are the shelter for all those who desperately longing to serve you. Hence please get up from sleep. We know you are big and took birth as a baby to bless us all.

निवास शय्यासन पादुकांशु कोपधान
वर्षातपवारणादिभिः
शरीरभेदैस्तव शेषतांगथैः यथोचितम् शेष इतीर्यते
जनैः (stotraratnam)

వాసపాదుక వసన శయ్యాసనేప
టర్థ పర్యంక వర్షాత పత్రములుగ
నుపకరించుచు నీకు యథోచితముగ
కొలువు సలిపెడి యా వేయితలల జేడు (My Yatirajiyam)

The Gopika girls are now trying to wake up Balarma. Oh! Balarama! You are invincible. You are the very source of all the strengths. As Balarama, you were uprooting the Hastinapuram along with river Yamuna, with your instrument. Your strength is immeasurable. *sem por kazhaladich chelvaa* The golden bangle you are wearing on your leg indicates who you are. How can you be sleeping? Please, you too, wake up. You have to get up and be there to help your brother, Krishna, in protecting all the devotees. Thus the girls are trying to wake up little Balarama.

Pasuram:

కడుపున కన్నంటు, మడుపులు గట్టను,
త్రావ నీరము నిచ్చు దానశొండ
మా రాజు, నిదుర లెమ్మా నందగోపాల

కోమలాంగులలోన, గొమిరెమిన్న,
మాకులదీపమా మా స్వామినీ యశో
దా దేవి! సుప్రభాతమ్ము లెమ్ము
నింగిదూటుచు పొంగ నంగమ్ము వెంచి లో
కాల(గొల్చిన పగకా(డ మింటి
ద్రిమ్మరీడుల యెకిమీ(డ దేవకీ కు
మార! మేల్కొనుమయ్య బంగారుగండ
పెండరము కాలివాడ, తమ్ముండు నీవు
మేలుకొనుమయ్య బలదేవ! మేలుకొనుము.

PASURAM 18

Introduction:

As the saying, 'नीलातुंग स्तनगिरितटी सुप्तम्' goes, Lord Krishna who is sleeping comfortably in the embrace of Neela Devi. Considering it is difficult to wake him up when he is in her strong embrace, Gopika Girls are now waking Neela Devi so that Krishna also can get up.

உந்து மத களிற்றன் ஓடாத தோள் வலியன்
    நந்தகோபாலன் மருமகளே! நப்பின்னாய்!
கந்தம் கமழும் குழலீ! கடைதிறவாய்
    வந்தெங்கும் கோழி அழைத்தன காண்! மாதவிப்
பந்தல் மேல் பல்கால் குயில் இனங்கள் கூவின காண்
    பந்தார் விரலி! உன் மைத்துனன் பேர் பாட
செந்தாமரைக் கையால் சீரார் வளையொலிப்ப
    வந்து திறவாய் மகிழ்ந்து ஏல் ஓர் எம்பாவாய்

Undhu madha kalitran Odaadha thol valiyan

Nandhagopan marumagalae nappinnaay

Kandham kamazhum kuzhali kadai thiravaay

Vandhu engum kozhi azhaiththana kaan maadhavip-

Pandhal mael pal kaal kuyilinangal koovina kaan

Pandhu aar virali un maiththunan paer paadach

Chendhaamaraik kaiyaal seeraar valai olippa

Vandhu thiravaay magizhndhaelor embaavaay (18)

Lord Krishna killed the fierce bulls, like Surabhasura, who were none other than the demons. This act was treated as kanya sulkam (unkuva=reverse dowry/kanya sulkam) Kumban gave the hand of Neela Devi to Krishna.

Meaning: Neela Devi is the daughter of Krishna's uncle, Kumba (brother of Yasoda Devi). When Krishna killed the fierce bulls like Surabhasura, the demons sent by Kamsa to terrorize the Gokul village, as a reward, His uncle offered him the hand of Neela Devi. Gopika girls find Lord Krishna is now sleeping under a tight embrace of Neela Devi. To get Him out of her strong embrace so that He could wake up, Gopika Girls decided to wake her up first. In the process, He could also get up. But, it is not possible to wake her up without her blessings.

Oh! Neela Devi! You are the daughter-in-law of Nanda Gopala, one who is also very strong as he has many head-strong elephants under his control. Krishna has acquired many great qualities from his father. Hence He is also powerful like his father. When Krishna was young, using his strength, He brought under his control the ferocious-looking Rakshas, like Surabhasura, who came in the form of bulls to terrorize the people. Krishna killed all of them. As a fitting reward, he won Neela Devi's hand.

Oh! Devi! You have imprisoned by your love, even the conqueror of those demons with your soft hands that look like lotus stems. Please have some mercy on us and release Him from your hands by waking up. Even after that request, she remained unresponsive while little of her movement caused the flowers that she tied to her hair emanated pleasing smells.

kandham kamazhum kuzhali kadai thiravaay, Oh! Mother! Neela Devi (*Nappinna piraatti!*), You may think that we do not see you awake. The beautiful kabarieebhara flowers decorating your hair are slowly falling to the ground due to your movement. We could smell their fragrance filling the room and even spreading outside through the windows. Please wake up. How long do you want to enjoy alone the presence of the Lord?

It is not one, and it is not at one place, 'engum kozhi' the Roasters all got up and making noise waiting for your appearance. The cuckoos you groomed have also gotten up, making roaring noises and waiting to see you. They have claimed canopies made up of Guruvinda creeps and making their 'kuhuu' sounds calling everyone to come. It is already getting late. It is not time for you to sleep anymore. Maybe you slept after getting tired from playing ball with your beloved at night.

At least now you can get up and open the doors with your delicate hands as the bangles you are wearing making 'gala gala' noise when they move. We girls have come here to sing the glories of your beloved and be compassionate and open the doors for us.

Implied meaning: One has to approach the Lord, keeping 'Piraatti' in front. The one who kept Seeta away, like Surpanaka, could not get a blessing from Lord Rama. On the other hand, Kakasura, once he fell at the feet of

Seeta for his mistake, was blessed by Rama. Hence to get protection from the Lord, one has to approach Him through Shree or Lakshmi. Hence the Vaishnavas are called Shree Vaishnavas as Shree comes first before approaching Lord Vishnu.

'Om' kaara is explained in the Vishistadvaita tradition as it stands for the three letters – अ + उ + म् . The letter अ stands for Vishnu – अक्षरानाम् अ कारोम्सि – one meaning is among the letters, I am the letter अ. उ – kaaro Lakshmi vaachakaH - उ stand for Laksmi and makaaro (म्) jeeva vaachakaH – the म् stands for Jeeva. Jeeva has to approach Lord Vishnu only via उ – Lakshmi. Lakshmi is the mother of all. The Jeeva, who has become dirty by playing in the world, cannot approach the father directly. He can always approach the mother. When he approaches his mother, she cleans the child first and ensures he is all clean before presenting him to the father. Mother is generally more tolerant than the father. म् letter is the 25th letter in the consonants in Indian languages. 24 entities designate Jeeva; pancha bhutas (five fundamental elements), pancha koshas (five sheaths – annamaya, etc) , pancha jnaanedriyas (five sense organs), pancha karmendriyas (five organs of action), and four inner instruments, mind, intellect, memory and ego – with total 24. The one who possesses these is the 25th one Jeeva, designated by the 25th letter म् . Thus Om-kaara indicates the method of solvation for a Jeeva, as per Shree Vaishnava's tradition.

ప్రత్యగానందునిన్ పరమపురుషుని
ప్రణవ స్వరూపునిన్ ట్రవచించు చుండు
నా యకా రోకారములు మకారమును
ఒండింట నోదిగిన యొంకార మిద్ది
యెద్ది వాకోన యోగికీఙన్మమృత్యు
సంసారబంధంటు సమసిపోయెడిని|| (My Prapanna Jana
Paatheyamu)

If you only go after Laksmi (wealth) without Vishnu (without spiritual mind), she will blast you. It happened to Ravana. He kidnapped Sita because of his hatred for Rama, and he got destroyed. Sita always stays with Rama, and she is the embodiment of noble and auspicious qualities. Vishnu carries Laksmi all the time in His Koustubha mani. Hence He is called Laksmi pati – ह्रीस्छते लक्ष्मीस्च पत्नौ -says Purusha Suktam. Lakshmi stands for Prakruti. Hence through Prakriti, Jeeva has to realize the Purusha, the Lord Vishnu.

The one who respected both Sita and Ram, Vibhishana, ultimately obtained all that Ravana owned. Hence in the Sharnagati gadyam, Shree Ramanuja first worshipped Shree Devi and, with her blessings, worshiped the Lord and thus got blessed.

Hence Jeevas should approach Shreeman Narayana properly with devotion and enjoy eternal happiness in His abode.

Pasuram:

మదపుటేనుగుల గములో మర్దింప(జాలిన
అర్గళ దీర్ఘబాహో విలాసు
శ్రీ నందగోపుని మేనగోడల సొగ
నిగుల వలపుల సెఱులదాన
నీలాసతీదేవి! కోలాహలము సేయు
కొక్కురోకో యంచు కోళ్ళగుంపు
గురివిందపందిరి కొననెక్కి కుహుకుహూ
కుహుయంచు కోయిలలో గూయ(దొడగె
కందుకమునాడి యలసిన కన్నెమిన్న
నిదుర లేలెమ్ము కీర్తింప నీదుప్రియుని
తలుపుదీయుము కెందామరలను బోలు
కరతలమ్ముల నులియంగ(గంకణములు.

PASURAM 19

Introduction:

The Gopika Girls are waking up both Neela Devi and Krishna.

குத்து விளக்கெரியக் கோட்டுக்கால் கட்டில் மேல்
    மெத்தென்ற பஞ்ச சயனத்தின் மேலேறி
கொத்து அலர் பூங்குழல் நப்பின்னை கொங்கைமேல்
    வைத்துக் கிடந்த மலர் மார்பா! வாய் திறவாய்
மைத்தடங் கண்ணினாய் நீயுன் மணாளனை
    எத்தனை போதும் துயில் எழ ஒட்டாய் காண்
எத்தனையேலும் பிரிவாற்ற கில்லையால்
    தத்துவம் அன்று தகவு ஏல் ஓர் எம்பாவாய்

Kuththu vilakkeriya kottuk kaal kattil mael

Meththenra pancha sayanaththin mael aerik

Koththalar poonguzhal nappinnai kongai mael

Vaiththuk kidandha malar maarbaa vaay thiravaay

Maith thadam kanninaay nee un manaalanai

Eththanai podhum thuyilezha ottaay kaan

Eththanaiyaelum pirivu aatragillaayaal

Thaththuvam anru thagavaelor embaavaay (19)

Meaning: While the light-pillars are shining brightly, the cot legs, made up of elephants' tusks, and softness, coolness, and comfort-ness emanating with the purity and beauty of Neela Devi's touch, are all very pleasing to the see. While the fragrant smells all around, with her soft hair spreading all over, Oh! Lord, you are sleeping comfortably using Neela Devi's upper body as a soft pillow. Can you please listen to our desperate pleas?

Thus Gopika girls, while reminding the Lord of His promise and recognizing without the consent of Neela Devi Lord is not going to respond, are trying again to wake her up. Oh! Mother! Neela Devi, who has applied kajal to eyelashes for beauty, lids, you have slept with your beloved holding tightly in your embrace and not letting Him go. Can't you bear the separation for a short time when He wakes up and leaves your bedroom to bless the other devotees waiting for Him? Like you, many are waiting to experience the Lord. Can you let them also have some happiness they get by serving Him? Please release Him from your embrace for some time, so He can come out and bless the other devotees.

Implied Meaning: Neela Devi is cited as an example of how one can get the greatest blessings from the Lord by serving him fully with the body, speech, and mind. It also indicates that Lord's blessing can be obtained only with the blessings of those Jeevas who have become very close to the Lord by their service. Neela Devi, Vishvaksena, Aadisheha, Garuda, etc., are ever-liberated souls (Nityamuka Jeevas). Serving them is similar to serving the Lord. Neela Devi's example illustrates that uniting with the Lord (Sayujya Mukti) becomes the final goal of all Jeeves and is the fulfillment of human life.

It also indicates that once one has reached the abode of the Lord, Jeeva does not bare to have a separation from Him even for a second. Also, Goda Devi says that the exalted happiness one gets in association with the Lord, when shared with others, will result in more happiness.

Not only that, serving the Lord without desiring any fruits of the action, remembering the lotus feet of the Lord, and performing and doing any action that is dharmic and offering the results of the actions at the holy feet of the Lord – forms the very purpose of life itself for of a devotee. Hence Krishna says,

यत् करोषि यत् अश्नासि, यत् जुहोषि ददासि यत्।
यत् तपस्यसि कौन्तेय तत् कुरुष्व मदर्पणम्॥
(Geeta 9:27)

Thus, whatever one does, eats, or performs yagnas, meditates, thus everything one does offer it to Me says the Lord. Of course, the Lord will accept it only if it is dharmic action. One cannot steal something and offer that to Him – He will not accept it. Meditation, and thus everything that one does should be worthy enough to offer it to Me, says the Lord. In addition, the results of all actions that were performed should also be offered at the feet of the Lord. In addition, Krishna says one should act only that is in tune with his Gunas and lineage and dictated by dharma shastras, 'स्वे स्वे कर्मण्यभिरत

स्संसिद्धिम् लभते नरः" (Geeta 18:45). One should act with a prayerful attitude and intelligently using the Lord-given intelligence.' स्वकर्मणा तमभ्यर्च्य सिद्धिम् विंदति मानवः' (Geeta 18:46) By performing the action that is Intune with his nature one can have a peaceful life and also attain the highest if it is done in a prayerful attitude.

If the assigned duties due to family lineage appear to be inappropriate from the point of others, one should not discard them, Also one should not take up others' duties that may look appropriate at the outset. Hence Geeta says:

श्रेयान् स्वधर्मो विगुण: परधर्मो त्स्वनुष्टितात्,
स्वभाव नियतम् कर्म कुर्वन्नाप्नोति किल्बिषम्।
सहजम् कर्म कौतेय सदोषमपि न त्यजेत्।
सर्वारम्भा हि दोषेण् धूमेनाग्निरिवावृता॥
(Geeta 48-18:47)

One should not take up the actions sanctioned for others even if they appear to be dharmic. It is better to do only actions that are assigned because of one's guna and birth, even if they appear to be inappropriate from the outside. This is because 'सर्वारंभा हि दोषेण धूमेनाग्नि रिवावृता: in every action there will always be some inappropriateness from some other reference. Hence, the actions that are in tune with one's heritage or lineage are done with an attitude of service to the Lord, without any selfish motives, then the Lord will be pleased.

Thus, if one with single-pointed devotion prays to the Lord, even if it appears that the Lord is otherwise busy, He will come running, leaving everything, to protect His devotees, as He has done to save Gajendra.

Pasuram:

కంటాల దీపాలు కాంతులీనగ దంత
    పల్యంకమున మేలి పాన్పుమీద
నిర్ఝారిగంధవన్నిత్య నూతన సుమ
    గుచ్ఛశోభిత నీలకుంత లాడ్య
పీవరోరోజ నప్పిన్నపిరాట్టి కు
    చ ద్వయాలీన విశాలవక్ష
నీవేని పల్కరాదా వాయి యరవిచ్చి
    కాటుకదిద్దిన కంటిదాన
వల్లభుని నొక్కక్షణమైన పడక విడిచి
వెడల నీయవె? విగడియ విరహామేని
తాళలే వింత స్వార్థము తగునె? పూరు
షోత్తముని నీ వొకర్తుక గుత్తగొంటె?

PASURAM 20

Introduction:

In this pasuram, Gopika girls are waking both Neela Devi and Lord Krishna.

முப்பத்து மூவர் அமரர்க்கு முன் சென்று
    கப்பம் தவிர்க்கும் கலியே! துயிலெழாய்
செப்பமுடையாய், திறலுடையாய் செற்றார்க்கு
    வெப்பம் கொடுக்கும் விமலா! துயிலெழாய்
செப்பன்ன, மென்முலை செவ்வாய் சிறுமருங்குல்
    நப்பின்னை நங்காய்! திருவே! துயிலெழாய்
உக்கமும் தட்டொளியும் தந்துன் மணாளனை
    இப்போதே எம்மை நீராட்டு ஏல் ஓர்
    எம்பாவாய்முப்பத்து

Muppaththu moovar amararkku mun senru

Kappam thavirkkum kaliyae thuyil ezhaay

Seppam udaiyaay thiral udaiyaay setraarkku-

Veppam kodukkum vimalaa thuyil ezhaay

Seppenna men mulaich chevvaaych chiru marungul

Nappinnai nangaay thiruvae thuyil ezhaay

Ukkamum thattoliyum thandhu un manaalanai

Ippodhae emmai neeraattaelor embaavaay (20)

Meaning: Oh! Paramatma! Morning Salutations to you! You are the protector of those who have surrendered to you. You have committed yourself to protect all saintly people. When the Rakshasas are trying to hurt the thirty-three types of Gods who have committed to following the dharmic path, you try to protect them without their even asking. You make the enemies of Dharma tremble by your strength. You promised to help those who surrendered to you and always keep your word. Based on your promise, we have come here after bathing in the cold water in the early morning. How come you, however much we call, are pretending to sleep? Is that fair on your part?

Oh! Mother *Nappinna Piratti*! 'seppenna men mulaich chevvaaych chiru *marungul*' by unparalleled exquisite beauty with every part of your body fully decorated appropriately and pleasing with smiling face, along with your natural beauty, your attractive posture, and style, you have mesmerized the Lord with your grace and beauty, and not allowing Him to come out by keeping quietly for yourself. Please have mercy on us, release the Lord from your embrace, and wake him up as many of his devotees are eager to be blessed by Him.

Please wake Him up after keeping the required beautiful mirror and auspicious smelling decorative herbs and ointments close by. Please be kind to us and bless us so our prayers will be successful.

Implied Meaning:

There are supposed to be 33 core devatas whom you can protect easily. On that scale, it is not really difficult to protect us as we are a much smaller number. Most devatas are males. They are divine and are also cable of defending themselves. They are powerful to rule over different parts of the universe. You took birth as a short young boy (vamana) to protest these powerful people. To do that, you even left your magnificent abode in Vaikunta.

In contrast, we are small village girls who have full faith in you. We are not powerful like the devatas, do not have that much energy to protect ourselves, and have no solace other than you. Can you not be kind to us? To punish the wicked, you came yourself leaving your Vaikunta. You took birth in the Nanda Gopala family due to their many merits in their past lives. As a small side action, can you not fulfill our desires and protect us? You went to protect the gods even before they asked you.

On the other hand, we have been standing in front of your room for hours and requesting you to get up and bless us. Can you not be compassionate with us? You never go back on your words, as you have proved before. You have made a promise that

सर्वधर्मान् परित्यज्य मामेकम् शरणम् व्रज।
अहम् त्वा सर्वपापेभ्यो मोक्षयिष्यामि मा शुचः॥
(Geeta 18:66)

Have you forgotten your promises while staying in the tight embrace of Neela Devi? How come you are not responding even after listening to our pleas? At least you can glance at us from the corner of your eyes and at least smile at us.

Or are you worried that you are not able to get out of the embrace of Neela Devi?

'చిక్కడు సిరి కా(గిటిలో(
జిక్కడు సనకాదియోగి చిత్తాబ్జములన
చిక్కడు శ్రుతిలతికావల
జిక్కినతడు లీలన(దల్లిచేత తోలన| (Potana)

Thus you, who never get bound by anybody, if people come to know that you got bound in the embrace of Neela Divi, you will become a laughing stock.

'If you say, 'why should I come as soon as you girls call me? We are your devotees and have completely surrendered to you. You promised that you would always oblige and bless your devotees. You normally do not get caught by anybody, and yet 'చిక్కినతడు లీలన(దల్లిచేత తోలన' thus you got caught by your mother, Yasoda Devi, who tied you to the mortar. That shows your favoritism towards your mother and not to us. You have promised to those who have completely surrendered to you as 'त्वाम् मोक्षयिष्यामि. Now you cannot go back on us. Your statement 'seppam udaiyaay' will have no more meaning if you do not bless us.

You are the embodiment of maaya and beyond the clutches of Prakriti. Then how can the embrace of Neela Devi imprison you?

We have not approached any other God. We know that they are insignificant in front of you. What they can give also is insignificant. Where can they get the power to give? You said,

कामैस्तैस्तैः हृतज्ञानाः प्रपद्यन्ते अन्यदेवताः
(Geeta 7:20)
लभते च ततः कामान् मयैव विहितान् हितान्॥
(Geeta 7:22)

Thus, even the power to give anything by them comes from Me only. Hence we do not go to them and offer ourselves.

నిన్నె నే శరణంటి నాదుభవమున్
నీ భారమే యంటి య
న్ము న్నైవేడను, నీకె సేవకు(డ
నన్నున్ బాలలో ముంచినా
మున్నీటన్ బడద్రోసినా యది
యశమ్మొ నిందయో నీకె యా
పన్నా నీకశరణ్య కీర్తికి(దగన్
వర్తింపుమో కేశవా| (My Keshavaprapatti)

"We are gods. We do possess some powers. We can use our strength to win over our enemies. We can easily dupe them and deceive them using unparallel weapons like 'acchar' (heavenly beauties)', they may proclaim. Yet to protect even these gods, you took various forms to destroy the Rakshasas. If you can protect those with powers, why are you not listening to our prayers? Unlike these gods, we are, by nature, very weak. How come you are not listening to our pleas?

When you could rush leaving everything and even dragging the upper cloth of Laksmi who was serving you at that time, 'శ్రీకుచోపరిచేలాంచలమైన వీడక' (Potana), to save Gajendra when he prayed for you, how come you are ignoring us even though we gave everything to serve you.

Thus, the Gopika girls try to wake up the Lord, and as unsuccessful, they return to Neela Devi to wake her up first.

Oh! Mother! Your beauty is unparalleled and unprecedented. Goddess Lakshmi is praised by saying, 'चैतन्यस्तन्य दायिनी, 'similarly, you are also holding as a mother, the divine milk that helps to propel the spiritual growth and prosperity of all Jeevas. With your close association with the Lord, the divine milk is purified and sacred for all of us. You are holding the Lord so dear to you with your beauty and devotion. As a result, Oh! Mother! Your milk not only sustains the life of all Jeeves but also carries, in its essence, the divine grace of the Lord. Oh! Great Mother! Without your blessings, we cannot approach the Lord.

त्वत्संप्रीत्यै विहरति हरौ सम्मुखीनाम् श्रुतीनाम् भावारूढौ भगवतियुवाम् दंपती दैवतम् नः (Shree Stuthi- Vedanta Desika)

Thus, for your happiness only, Bhagavan is projecting this wonderful world as part of His Leela. You both together are our Gods. Without worshiping you first, we cannot even approach the Lord, who is the final goal for our salvation. We want to surrender to you first before we approach the Lord. Neela Devi, you are our solace. Please wake up from sleep so that we can serve and then the Lord.

Hence Oh! Devi! After waking up Bhagavan and bringing all the required accessories for doing Lord's prayer, please send Him to us for the completion of our ritual. He is the presiding deity for our yagna or ritual. Not only that,

"अहम् क्रतु रहम् यज्ञः स्वधाऽहमहमौषधम्|
मंत्रोऽह मह मेवाज्य महमग्नि रहम् हुतम्" (Geeta 9:16))

Lord says He is yagna, He is the materials that are used in the yagna, He is the ghee that is offered into the yagna, He is the mantram that is chanted while doing yagna – in essence, He is everything. When He is everything, how can we do anything? Oh! Mother! Without His blessings. Hence, we request you kindly wake Him up and send Him here so we can do our ritual prayer.

Oh! Mother! You are an intermediary between Bhagavan and us. The ones you want thattoliyum (a large mirror) and ukkamum (special decorative circular fan - Alavattam) are not external objects. The mirror we request is ashtakshari (eight letter) mantram, and Alavattamu is a two letter mantram (dvayam).

The mirror only shows the objects that are external to the mirror, while the ashtakshari mantram clearly shows the supreme eternal divine objects. In the universe, there are two types of materials, chit, and achit, that is, conscious and unconscious entities. Of the conscious entities, there are again two; one is jeevas, and the other is Paramatma. The indestructible or eternal entities are indicated by the letter Na Ra – in the Narayana Mantram.

'riij' means that which gets destroyed or changes, derived from the root ' raH', meaning that which changes or undergoes destruction. Na letter negates; hence 'na ra' means things that do not get destroyed. These include Prakruti and Jeevas, which are part of Him. The eternal divine objects are designated by Nara. Ayanam means shelter. Hence Narayana means the one who is a shelter to the Prakruti and Jeevas. Thus in the ashtottaram mantram, 'Om Namo Narayana!' – Narayana denotes the abode or shelter for the eternal, indestructible entities in the Universe. The shelter is different from the one that provides the Shelter- This includes Bhagavan and Adi Laksmi. Hence Nara includes only Prakruti and Jeevas.

In His teaching to Arjuna, Krishna starts with the statement that you are crying where there is no reason to cry. It is because nobody really dies – 'अजोनित्यम् शास्वतोयम् पुराणो' – The so-called death is like changing worn out clothes.' नत्वेवाहम् जातुनासम् न त्वम् नेमे जनाधिपा:' – there was never a time I was not there, nor you, nor all these kings that are standing in front. Prakruti is also beginningless. It is described as 'अजामेकाम् लोहितशुक्ल कृष्णाम्,' meaning the Prakriti with its three Gunas, sattva, rajas and tamo gunas and has no beginning – thus creation-sustenance-and destruction is a continuous cycle without beginning and hence no end also.

Krishna goes into more detail about the nature of Prakriti and Jeeves. My prakruti is of eight fold or eight aspects, मे प्रकृतिरष्टधा – Different from Prakruti is the chit aspect- 'अपरेयमितस्त्वन्याम् प्रकृतिम् विद्धिमेपराम् जीवभूताम्'. Of the Jeevas there are three types, nitya, baddha, and mukta (eternal, bound and free), "जहात्येनाम् भुक्तभोगामजोन्यः Jeevas that experience as per their karmas the inert (achit), and the once who after surrendering to the Lord have reached His abode (mukta Jeevas) and those that are eternal unbound Jeevas like Neela Devi, Garuda, Vishvaksena, etc who are serving the Lord all the time. Thus all indestructible Jeevas and Prakruti are designated by the word 'na ra' in the Narayana mantra.

Narayana mantram is done with Om-kaara. अ in Om designates Vishnu and उ in Om designates Lakshmi Devi. म्-kaara refers to the Jeevas. 'अकारार्थो विष्णुः – मकारार्थो जीवः'-says Ashta Sloki. namaH in the mantra indicates that Jeevas surrender ('na ma' – not me – I am not a separate entity that I thought I was, and I am surrendering myself completely and hence no me anymore). Thus Om Namo Naarayanaya – mantra designates complete surrender of the Jeeva at the feet of the Lord Narayana. Hence it is called muula mantam, or fundamental mantra to be obtained from the Acharya, who himself has surrendered to the Lord.

Thus, the Narayana mantra indicates the sharanagati path for Jeevas. To indicate the path of sharanagati, to liberate from both cause and effect duality, contributing to the bondage of all Jeevas, that goal – *ukkamum* - the Gopika girls here requesting in '*ukkamum thattoliyum thandhu un*'.

Pasuram:

మున్నుగా వేంచేసి ముప్పదిమూ(డు కో
       టుల యమరుల భీతి తొల(గ(ద్రోయ(
బాలింప దీనుల(జాలిన యౌదార్య
       బలములు గలిగిన భద్రమూర్తి
పరిపంథులను భయం పరచు తేజశ్శాలి
       మేలుకోవయ్య మమ్మెలు కొనుము
టంగారు కుండల రంగారు వక్షోజ
       ములను నెన్నడుము కెమ్మోవి దాన
నిదుర లేవమ్మ సీమంతినీమతల్లి
ఆలవట్టము దెమ్ము నీలాపురంధ్రి
దర్పణము నిమ్ము నందనుని మమ్ము
చెలగి యిప్పుడు నీరాడ(జేయు మమ్మ.

PASURAM 21

Introduction:

The Gopika girls are waking up Lord Krishna

ஏற்ற கலங்கள் எதிர்பொங்கி மீதளிப்ப
    மாற்றாதே பால் சொரியும் வள்ளல் பெரும் பசுக்கள்
ஆற்றப் படைத்தான் மகனே! அறிவுராய்
    ஊற்றமுடையாய்! பெரியாய் உலகினில்
தோற்றமாய் நின்ற சுடரே! துயிலெழாய்
    மாற்றார் உனக்கு வலிதொலைந்து உன் வாசற்கண்
ஆற்றாது வந்து உன் அடி பணியுமாபோலே
    போற்றியாம் வந்தோம் புகழ்ந்து ஏல் ஓர் எம்பாவாய்

aetra kalangal edhir pongi meedhalippa

Maatraadhae paal soriyum vallal perum pasukkal

Aatrap padaiththaan maganae arivuraay

Ootram udaiyaay periyaay ulaginil-

Thotramaay ninra sudarae thuyil ezhaay

Maatraar unakku vali tholaindhu un vaasar kan

Aatraadhu vandhu un adi paniyumaa polae

Potriyaam vandhom pugazhndhaelor embaavaay (21)

Meaning: Oh! Lord! Even Vedas cannot describe your glories.

Your brilliance is equal to the brilliance of more than a thousand suns. Yet curtailing all your brilliance to a very tiny fraction of it so that our eyes look at you without any problem, you took the birth as Krishna to protect all of us. You are Paramatma born to bless us all. Oh! Lord! Our Salutations (suprabhatam) to you.

Just as your enemies, unable to fight with you or hide somewhere to escape from you, surrendered themselves at your feet to become your slaves, we also surrendered ourselves becoming slaves to your majestic beauty and magnificent culture. We have come here to glorify you and to receive your benedictions. Please get up from your sleep and bless us.

Implied meaning: Oh! Son of Nandaji! How many times do we have to try to wake you up? You are not responding to our calls. Even the girls, who depend on others, could get up after we called them just two times. You are a prince and will be taking full responsibility to protect others. Is it appropriate to sleep like a log?

Thinking that You are the son of Nandaji, who owns many cows as his property, putting an air of a prince, are you ignoring us? You are keeping silent, thinking that we are just village girls. Why are you not even looking at us and keeping silent? We are not really different people. We are part of Nanda Gopala's circle of relatives.

We did not trouble you by waking you up when you were in Vaikunta on the milky ocean, requesting you to come down to earth as Gods did, or praying you to come and save us like Gajendra. You have already come down to earth as an incarnation as Krishna and have stayed with us since we were children. Hence, out of your close association with us, we took the liberty to come and wake you up. Don't we have that much liberty to come and wake you up? And don't you want to oblige, get up and bless us?

We know the absolute truth of who you are and who we are. We know that you are the master, and we are your property. You are eternal, and we are part of you. You have said in Geeta, 'ममैवांशो जीवलोके जीवभूत स्सनातनः' that we are part of you. Since we are part of you and belong to you, is it not your responsibility to protect us? Does anyone have to remind you of this? If you do not protect your property, who will be looser?

'ootram udaiyaay periyaay ulaginil thotramaay ninra sudarae thuyil ezhaay', You are the supreme, and who are we to describe your greatness? You are beyond any description. Who are we, to talk about you?

तत्वेन यस्य महिमार्णव शीकराणुः शक्योसमातुमपि शर्वपितामहाद्यैः
कर्तुं तदीयमहिमस्तुति मुद्यताय महयन्नमोऽस्तु कवये निरपत्रपाय॥ (Shree Yamunacharya)

When Vedas and Gods, Brahma, Rudra, Sanaka Sanada, etc., could not describe you, who are we to describe and praise?

You are born to uplift Dharma and protect the sages. Ok! You have come down to earth and taken birth as a human. Yet who can stand to face your brilliance?

दिवि सूर्य सहस्रस्य भवेद्युगपदुत्थिता।
यदि भाः सदृशी सा स्यात् भासस्तस्य महात्मनः॥
(Geeta 11:12))

You are more brilliant than thousands of suns; how can anybody see you? The sun and moon are nothing compared to your brilliance.

भीषास्माद्वातः पवते, भीषोदेति सूर्यः (Sruti)

Thus even the sun and moon, out of fear for you, are doing their assigned duties without fail. Being such brilliance, how can any human being stand? Hence you had curtained all your brilliance when you took birth as a human being. 'अवजानंति माम् मूढा मानुषीम् तनु माश्रितम्' (Geeta 11:9)– thus only those who are ignorant try to insult you. Only your devotees can guess your true nature, and not possible for others.

त्वाम् शीलरूपचरितैः परमप्रकृष्टैः
सत्वेन सात्विकतया प्रबलैश्च शास्तैः
प्रख्यात दैवपरमार्थ विदाम् मतैश्च
नैवासुर प्रकृतयः प्रभवंति बोद्धुम्॥ (Shree Yamunacharya)

Only those with predominant sattva guna can learn the shastras that describe your glories and not others who are engulfed with tamo and rajo gunas. Even the great sages were unable to determine the nature of the supreme Paramatma other than saying statements with 'neti (not this), neti (not this)' due to their inability to define you.

They could establish vaguely, to a small extent mentioning that You are Shiva, or Shakti or power, or so many other ways due to overpowering ignorance. Without completely surrendering to you, one cannot know you because of your maaya. They also need the grace of Goddess Maha Laksmi to approach you.

ह्रीश्चते लक्षीश्च पत्न्यौ – thus says shruti, indicates that you are the husband of Lakshmi. Thus, to identify you, they need to know first Goddess Lakshmi. Then they can recognize you as the husband of Goddess Lakshmi. Without her, they cannot approach you.

Yet, you have come down and taken birth here as Krishna to protect the world. Because of our good deeds, we can see you. Oh! Lord! Who are we to wake you up? Do you really sleep? Your sleep is 'meditative sleep' (yoga nidra) and not propelled by tamo guna, as in other beings.

कौसल्या सुप्रजा राम पूर्वा संध्या प्रवर्तते।
उत्तिष्ठ नरशार्दूल कर्तव्यम् दैवमाह्निकम्॥
(Ramayanam)

Thus Sage Viswamitra was trying to wake you up.

'I know Shree Ramachandra, 'अहम् वेद्मि महात्मानम्' -as the statement made by the Sage Viswamitra, yet he said, please get up to do ' दैवमाह्निकम्' (offering salutations to all Gods). Who is the one to perform the 'आह्निकम्' or morning prayers? The one who knows that Lord Rama is incarnate of Paramatma, yet he is trying to wake up Lord Rama to do prayers to other Gods. How can Viswamitra, who knows the truth that Rama himself is none other than Paramatma, can ask Rama to do morning prayers? Then how can Viswamitra be considered the knower of the truth?

Viswamitra has to do morning payers. That, too, the Gayatri mantram, revealed to the sage Viswamitra by Goddess Gayatri, has to be done by every human being qualified to do it. When the Lord is pretending to sleep, Vishwamitra has to pretend to wake Him up so he can do the morning prayers. Hence the deeper meaning of the Ramayana sloka is 'I am going to do the morning prayers, you, please get up and bless me, उत्तिष्ठ नरशार्दूल्.

In the same way, you are pretending that you are asleep with half-closed eyes. We want you to open your eyes fully and bless us. This way, we can sing 'Suprabhatam' to you. For that, we came and stood here desperately in the very early morning to serve your holy feet. Just as the enemies that you have defeated are now due to loss of all their strength are waiting at your gate, we are also waiting here not out of fear but out of reverence and devotion towards you and to offer our prayers to your holy feet. When you have the compassion to bless even these enemies, why are you ignoring us who have surrendered to you, considering you are the only goal we seek? It is also the plea of many Jeevas like us. You have promised to bless all who have completely surrendered to you.

Jeevas are only part of Bhagavan. One who is very brilliant deliberately decreased His otherwise unbearable brilliance and took birth as a human being by His own will to save those desperately seeking liberation and punish those who are causing suffering to others.

अजोऽपि सन्नव्ययात्मा भूतानामीश्वरोऽपि सन्।
प्रकृतिम् स्वामधिष्ठाय संभवाम्यात्म माययाll
(Geeta 4:6))

Hence the Jeevas who are seeking liberation from this cycle of birth and death have to leave their ego (I-ness) and possessiveness (my-ness) and have to surrender themselves completely at the feet of Bhagavan. They will obtain moksha as promised by the Lord.

Pasuram:

ఆ(క యొకింతలేక పట్టిన యన్ని
పాత్రలు నిండారి పైన పొరలి
పారునట్టుల పాలవర్షించు నావులు
గలవాని కొమరు(డా కన్నుదెరుము
రక్షింపభక్తుల శిక్షింప వైరుల
తేరిచూడగరాని తేజుపుడమి
రూపుగట్టిన యట్టులేపు సూపిన దేవ
మేలుకోవయ్య మమ్మెలుకొనుము
ఎదురుకొనలేక భుజబలమేది నీదు
పగఱు నీయింటి వాకిటి పంచ(టడిన
వడుపునన్ మిమ్ము సామి నీ యడుగుదామ
రలను పొగడెడి శరణాగతులను గనుము.

PASURAM 22

Introduction:

The Gopika girls are requesting Krishna's compassion and grace.

அங்கண் மா ஞாலத்து அரசர் அபிமான
    பங்கமாய் வந்து நின் பள்ளிக் கட்டிற்கீழே
சங்கமிருப்பார் போல் வந்து தலைப்பெய்தோம்
    கிண்கிணி வாய்ச் செய்த தாமரைப் பூப்போலே
செங்கண் சிறுச் சிறிதே எம்மேல் விழியாவோ
    திங்களும் ஆதித்தியனும் எழுந்தாற்போல்
அங்கண் இரண்டுங்கொண்டு எங்கள் மேல்
    நோக்குதியேல்
எங்கள் மேல் சாபம் இழிந்து ஏல் ஓர் எம்பாவாய்

Angkan maanyaalaththu arasar abimaana-

Pangamaay vandhu nin pallik kattir keezhae

Sangam iruppaar pol vandhu thalaippeydhom

Kingini vaaych cheydha thaamaraip poop polae

Sengan chiruch chiridhae emmael vizhiyaavo

Thingalum aadhiththanum ezhundhaar pol

Angkan irandum kondu engal mael nokkudhiyael

Engal mael saabam izhindhaelor embaavaay (22)

Meaning: The kings from different parts of the world, whose kingdoms are flourishing with abundance and prosperity and living in their spacious palaces, have given up their pride and surrendered themselves to you and are now waiting for your grace. Similarly, we are also waiting at your threshold as a group, leaving all our pride, ego, and sense of ownership wishing for your grace, considering you are the Lord of all Lords, and none is equal to you.

Please look at us with your smiling eyes. Your very look, incomparable to the luster of the sun and the moon, can wipe out all our sins and purify us completely.

Special meaning: In this world, people become Kings due to their merits in their past lives. They become lords of the empires, which can be very vast. Because of the wealth and prosperity, they become blind with pride and arrogantly think that they 'are superior to everybody and have earned the kingdom out of their valor and nobody is equal to them. With that arrogant attitude, they tried to impose their will on others and enslave others like Hiranyaaksha or Hiranyakashipu.

As the saying in Telugu, 'తాడితన్నువాని తలదన్నువాడుండు,' the ones who think they can kick others' heads, there will be another who can kick their heads. When they encounter the more powerful one, they must surrender themselves, losing all their pride and the empire.

The real truth is when we are born, we don't bring with us even an inch of land nor a piece of wealth with us, nay, not even a piece of cloth to cover us. We cannot take an iota of wealth when we leave this earth. We must leave everything for others to enjoy or for the Government to confiscate. It was said that when the so-called Alexander the great was dying, he asked to be buried with his open hands for others to see, indicating that he was not taking anything with him despite conquering other kingdoms.

'కారే రాజులు రాజ్యముల్ గలుగగపే? గర్వోన్నతిన్ బొందరే? వారేరీ? సిరిమూటగట్టుకొని పోవంజాలిరే? భూమిపై పేరైనన్ గలదే?...' (Potana Bhagavatam).

It says, ' were there not many kings, who have won kingdoms and reached the highest wealth in the world? What happened to all of them? Has any king been able to pack his wealth and take it with him when he died? We do not even remember their names. Hence, what is the use of being proud of the wealth that one possesses? What good is claiming that this is mine and that also I want to make it mine, etc., when we are not going to take anything with us when our time here is over?

వెంటవచ్చిన దేహా మిదె శాశ్వతము గాదు
అసువు లెడసిన పిదప(టుడమి నిలబడటోౕదు
అపుడే ఇపుడే దీనిగడువు తెలియగరాదు
ఆ పైన వగపు నీ కావంత కొరగాదు|| (My Prapanna Jana PaathEyamu)

The one who has created all this, and other worlds is Shreeman Narayana. During the 'pralaya' or desolution time, He absorbs this entire universe in Him in subtle form.

नारायणादेव समुत्पद्यंते
नारायणात्प्रवर्तंते नारायणे प्रलीयन्ते|
(Mahopanishat)

अहम् कृत्स्नस्य जगतः प्रभवः प्रळयस्तथा,
भूतग्राम स्स्येवायम् भूत्वा भूत्वा प्रलीयते
(Geeta 7:6)
रात्यागमेऽवशः पार्थः प्रभवत्यहरागमे||
(Geeta 8:19)

Thus all that you have is His. He is the real owner, and everything in this universe belongs to Him. The feelings that this is mine and that is mine are imaginations or illusions in the mind since we came with nothing and we have to leave everything. Hence feelings like I am the owner of all this wealth and property or land and no one is superior to me, etc., are like the claims made by Hiranyaksha or Hiranyakashipu – in the end, Lord took it away along with their lives.

Hence the feelings of I-ness (ahankara or ego) and my-ness (mamakara or notion that all this is mine) only contribute to one's degradation as they are not real. Any individual or Jeeva himself belongs to Him. Hence it is better to surrender to His holy feet as that is where a Jeeva belongs.

Thus on those who recognize the above facts and surrender completely, He pours out His compassion, which can be seen by His compassionate looks.

The sun and the moon form his eyes. He emits the luster that is intolerable to look for His enemies while He makes it pleasing for His devotees.

Since the Gopika girls are His devotees, they need pleasing glances of the Lord. Hence they indicate the moon as *'Thingalum aadhiththanum ezhundhaar pol'*

Since compassionate looks of the Lord destroys all the sins of His devotees that obstruct their attaining the moksha and bless them with the eternal happiness they are longing for.

Just by the dust of His feet, if Ahalya Devi attained moksha. Then, as the saying goes 'सर्वेंद्रियाणाम् नयनम् प्रधानम्, of all the sense organs the eyes are most important, we cannot imagine what His compassionate glances with His eyes will do for His devotees. How can we describe the fortune of devotees immersed in His compassionate glances?

What more do these devotees want? What they get is incomparable with all the wealth in the world that one can get. Their happiness is beyond any ananda scale. Hence it is essential to utilize the blessed birth as a human being and renounce all the sense-pleasures and the desire to possess material wealth and prosperity, and devote time to prayers and service of the Lord.

Pasuram:

విపులావనీనాథులవగత గర్వులై
గుమిగూడి నీదు కంకటిక క్రింద
మూ(గినట్టుల మేము ముదిత లెల్లరు చేరి
నీ పాద సన్నిధి నిలచినాము
చిఱుతగజ్జలువోలె చెన్నొందు కెంపుదా
మరలు నా దరవికస్వరవిలోచ
నాంచలమ్ముల కాంతు లించుక మాపయి
ప్రసరింప(జేయుమా పంకజాక్ష
వేడి వెలు(గును జల్లని వెలుగుటో(లు
రెండు కన్నులసెండ రేయెండ గురిసి
మమ్ము(గరుణించితేని యస్మత్సమస్త
పాప సంచయములు పటాపంచ లగును.

PASURAM 23

Introduction:

Son of Nanda, while still lying on the bed, opening his eyes, asked the Gopika girls what they wanted. The girls are responding.

மாரிமலை முழைஞ்சில் மன்னிக் கிடந்து உறங்கும்
    சீரிய சிங்கம் அறிவுற்றுத் தீவிழித்து
வேரி மயிர்ப்பொங்க எப்பாடும் பேர்ந்து உதறி
    மூரி நிமிர்ந்து முழங்கிப் புறப்பட்டுப்
போதருமா போலே நீ பூவைப் பூவண்ணா உன்
    கோயில் நின்று இங்ஙனே போந்தருளி, கோப்புடைய
சீரிய சிங்காசனத்திலிருந்து, யாம் வந்த
    காரியம் ஆராய்ந்து அருள் ஏல் ஓர் எம்பாவாய்

Maari malai muzhainchil mannik kidandhu urangum

Seeriya singam arivutruth thee vizhiththu

Vaeri mayir ponga eppaadum paerndhu udhari

Moori nimirndhu muzhangip purappattup

Podharumaa polae nee poovaippoo vannaa un-

Koyil ninru ingnganae pondharulik koppudaiya-

Seeriya singaasanaththu irundhu yaam vandha-

Kaariyam aaraayndhu arulaelor embaavaay (23)

Meaning: In the rainy season, King Lion, while staying inside his cave and sleeping fearlessly, after hearing the thunder and got up irritated due to the sound, angry and ferocious for getting disturbed from a sound sleep, came out of the cave to punish the culprit, not finding anyone there who made the noise, shook his head spreading his hair, stretching himself and went out to ignoring little animals here and there and claimed his majestic thrown, which is at way high level. In the same way, Gopicas are picturizing Lord Krishna's situation.

Oh! Little Lion of Nandaji, who is sleeping on Neela Devi's body with head between her bosom, and after getting up and stretching the body, opening the lotus-like eyes, look at us with your eyes, which look slightly reddish due to extended love play with Neela Devi in the night. May we also be fortunate to see and enjoy your beauty, just as Neela Devi did.

Listening to those pleadings of the Gopika girls, "disregarding the time or place, is it appropriate for you all to barge in like this? Is it proper manners?" when Nanda Nandana asked, the girls responded.'Swami, please do not get angry with us. Please excuse us, as we are your children. न खलु निजशिशूनाम् सन्निधिर्वीड हेतुः (Lakshmi Sahasram), is there an inappropriate time for children to see their parents? Why is it inappropriate for us to come and see you as we are your children? What is the objection for us to seeing you here? Those of us who got caught up with the people entangled in the clutches of Prakrit and desperately crying, unable to tolerate separation from you – what are the allowed times for us to come to you? We could not bear the suffering of being caught in the Samsara and came back to you for forgiveness and solace.

Krishna asks, 'OK! You have come. Still, My sleep got disturbed. What do you girls want from me?' If you ask like that, then;

'Swami! How can you listen to our wishes while staying inside? Please come out like a lion so we can see your majestic walk, occupy your pedestal and listen to our requests.

How can you pay attention to our desperate cries when you are with your darling and enjoying her beauty and forgetting everything else? Once you have come out and occupied your majestic seat while enjoying your holy presence, which will relieve our physical and mental sufferings. We can then slowly express our desires for your consideration.

Implied meaning: There are no appropriate or inappropriate timings for Jeevas to reach the abode of Paramatma. 'तदेव लग्नम् सुदिनम् तदेव'.

తారా బలం చంద్ర బలం తదేవ

విద్యా బలం దైవ బలం తదేవ

లక్ష్మీపతేంఘ్రి యుగం స్మరామి

The best time will not be of much use regardless of how much wealth, fame, and name when you are obsessed with your desires and vasanas . These bring only misery without the grace of Lakshmi pati, Narayana.

When one has developed dispassion towards samsara, he has to renounce it immediately. There is a saying to that effect, 'यदहानि विरज्यंते तदहानि प्रव्रजेत्'.

He is Purushottam. He is responsible for the creation and sustenance of this entire universe. In trying to protect the creation, He is vigilant in punishing the wicked. Hence He is naturally very kind, compassionate, and considerate, He superimposes on Himself anger and looks at those who go against the Dharma with angry looks. Then His face is like the fierce sun with unbearable looks. At that time, it is very difficult to approach Him.

Hiranyakashipa without concerned about others, only indulging in selfish desires, and enjoying all the time sense objects, declaring himself 'अहम् ब्रह्मास्मि', I am the supreme Brahman, no one is above me, and concentrating only on his food and clothes and controlling everyone around. Since he has golden food and golden clothes, he is called Hiranyakashipu. He did not care for Paramatma. Both the brothers, Hiranyakashipu and Hiranyaakshu only interested in indulging in sense pleasures. People like them do not care about what is right and wrong and constantly indulge in activities that are adharmic and hurt others. Hence because of them, even the sages were hurt. Hence to kill them, the Lord took ferocious forms pretending to be very angry. During that time, even Gods are afraid to approach Him.

After looking at the ferocious form that Lord took to kill Hiranyakashipu, even Goddes Laksmi was hesitant to approach Him. Then, what to talk about ordinary people? Even the Gods went to see Him keeping the young boy, Prahalada, in front of them, knowing that Narasima would not be angry with the child-devotee.

Hence we need to approach Him, keeping His devotees in front so that He glances at us also with His kind and considerate looks.

For those blessed by His compassion, His looks will be comfortable like the rays of a cold moon. Just as the clear crystal looks red near the red flower, near the adharmic people, He looks fiery. Once they are removed, His natural pleasing and compassionate looks, pleasant smile, and lotus eyes projecting divine light become apparent.

When He occupies His majestic throne, a divine environment gets projected. The compassion to bless and fulfill the desires of His devotees and His large-heartedness get projected. The blessings the devotees receive at that time are auspicious and unparallel, and fulfilling.

Pasuram:

వానల కాలాన పర్వతగుహలోన
　　నెమ్మది సింగంటు నిద్రగూరి
మేల్కొని, కనువిచ్చి మిరుమిట్లుగొల్పు చూ
　　పుల నెల్లదిక్కుల(గలయ(జూచి
మెయి నిక్క గదలించి మెడజూలు విదిలించి
　　గర్జించి వెడలంగ గడిగినట్లు
పడకటింటిని వీడి పంచాస్యగతితోడ
　　నరుదెంచి మేలి సింహాసనమున.
అవిసెపూవన్నె తిరుమేనియందగా(డ
　　కొలువుదీరుము; వచ్చిన గోపకన్ని
యల విచారించి కోరిక లవధరించి
　　నీవు కరుణింపు మమ్ము సింహవలగ్న|

PASURAM 24

Introduction:

Gopika girls are surrendering themselves to Lord Krishna

அன்று இவ்வுலகம் அளந்தாய் அடிபோற்றி
    சென்றங்குத் தென்னிலங்கை செற்றாய் திறல்
    போற்றி
பொன்றச் சகடமுதைத்தாய் புகழ் போற்றி
    கன்று குணிலா வெறிந்தாய் கழல் போற்றி
குன்று குடையா வெடுத்தாய் குணம் போற்றி
    வென்று பகை கெடுக்கும் நின்கையில் வேல்
    போற்றி
என்றென்றுன் சேவகமே ஏத்திப் பறை கொள்வான்
    இன்றுயாம் வந்தோம் இரங்கு ஏல் ஓர் எம்பாவாய்

Anru iv ulagam alandhaay adi potri

Senranguth thenilangai setraay thiral potri

Ponrach chakatam udhaiththaay pugazh potri

Kanru kunilaa erindhaay kazhal potri

Kunru kudaiyaay eduththaay gunam potri

Venru pagai kedukkum nin kaiyil vael potri

Enrenrum un saevagamae aeththip parai kolvaan

Inru yaam vandhom irangaelor embaavaay (24)

Meaning: To save the Gods, you, who, beyond the birth and death, by your will, took the birth as Vamana, to the blessed couple, Aditi and Kasyapu, because of their devotion and meditation on you.

The grandson of your devotee, Prahlada, the emperor Bali, to get rid of his ego (I-ness) and possessiveness (my-ness) and to purify him, using the pretext of helping Gods, with your three feet covered the entire universe. Our salutations to your sacred lotus feet.

Propelled by Kamsa, ShaTakasura Rakshasa, the one who came to Brindavan to kill all the children in this village in the form of a cart you have made into powder by kicking him with your feet. To those divine feet, our salutations.

In the same way, the demon, Vatsasura, who came in the form of a calf and mingled with the herd of calves, you throw him away as though he is just a wooden splinter, to you who is strongest one, our salutations.

When Devendra got angry with the villagers who started worshiping the Govardhana Hill, on your advice, instead of him as they were doing before and started pouring heavy rains to destroy the village and people, you, to protect the people, cows, and other living beings, you lifted the whole Govardhana hill and made it as an umbrella under which everyone can be saved for days. To your kindheartedness, our salutations.

Defeating all the enemies and destroying their head-strongness, ego, and possessiveness, you made all of them surrender to you. For your valor, our salutations.

In this way, singing your glories and waiting to see your divine face and receive your blessings and affection, wishing to get our desires for solvation and your protection, we, the Gukula girls hoping that your kind glances will be on us.

Pasuram:

జయమంగళము సామి జగములఁ గొలచిన
    యానాటి నీదు పాదాబ్జములకు
శుభమంగళము లంక జొచ్చి యా పొలదిండి
    దనుజులఁ జెండు దోర్దండములకు
శ్రీమంగళము టండిరేద్రిమ్మరిని మట్టు
    వెట్టిన నీ పాదఘుట్టనకును
దివ్యమంగళము దైతేయువత్సాకారు
    కట్టినా విసరిన టెట్టిదునకు
మాటకందని నీమహిమల నుతించి
వాంఛితార్థము వడయంగ వచ్చినాము
ఆతపత్రీకృతోన్నతాహార్య నీకు
మంగళము సర్వజేతకు మంగళమ్ము.

PASURAM 25

Introduction:

Gopika girls are praising Lord Krishna.

ஒருத்தி மகனாய்ப் பிறந்து ஓர் இரவில்
   ஒருத்தி மகனாய் ஒளித்து வளர
தரிக்கிலான் ஆகித்தான் தீங்கு நினைத்த
   கருத்தைப் பிழைப்பித்துக் கஞ்சன் வயிற்றில்
நெருப்பென்ன நின்ற நெடுமாலே உன்னை
   அருத்தித்து வந்தோம் பறை தருதியாகில்
திருத்தக்க செல்வமும் சேவகமும் யாம்பாடி
   வருத்தமும் தீர்ந்து மகிழ்ந்து ஏல் ஓர் எம்பாவாய்

Oruthi maganaay pirandhu Oriravil-

Oruthi maganaay oliththu valarath

Tharikkilaan aagith thaan theengu ninaindha

Karuththaip pizhaippiththuk kanchan vayitril

Neruppenna ninra nedumaalae!, unnai-

Aruththiththu vandhom parai tharudhiyaagil

Thiruththakka selvamum saevagamum yaam paadi

Varuththamum theerndhu magizhndhaelor embaavaay (25)

Meaning: What can we say about the meritorious fruits of their devotion to the supreme Lord? They can enjoy the divine plays of the Lord in the form of little Krishna, who became well known only as the son of Yasoda Devi and Nanda Baba.

Due to the terrible actions of Kamsa and to protect the little Krishna from the atrocities that the Rakshasas were committing at the instigation of Kamsa, Yasoda Devi and Nanda Baba took care of growing Krishna by trying to keep him a secret, *oliththu valarath,* just like hiding the very precious things from the robbers.

Even though Krishna was born as Kshatriya, he did not receive all the required Vedic rituals. What is the meaning of these rituals for Paramatma? The ritual to be performed after birth, naming ceremony, chanting of sahasranaams of the Lord, etc. Are they required for Paramatma?

That his death is ordained by the eighth son of Devaki and Vasudeva, Kamsa was determined to kill their babies as soon as they were born and was waiting for the delivery of the eighth baby. Due to the power of maaya of the Lord, Kamsa could not know what happened on the night when Krishna was born. Instead of the son expected for Devaki, Kamsa found that it was a girl but still tried to kill the baby. He failed in his attempt to kill the baby, as the baby sprung up into the sky and announced to Kamsa that the one who would kill him was already born in his kingdom. Kamsa listening to that, became furious and employed Rakshasa to kill all newborn babies in his kingdom. Because of Lord's power of Maaya, Kamsa did not know what really happened on the night when Krishna was born. The Rakshasas came to Gokula and tried to kill little Krishna. However, one by one, Kamsa sent failed in their attempts. Kamsa thus suspected Krishna was going to kill him and kept sending more powerful Rakshasas to kill little Krishna.

Until he hears about the death of little Krishna, Kamsa cannot even sleep and is losing his patience. All his attempts to kill Krishna became futile. That was causing more agitation and anxiety in Kamsa. Krishna may be causing Kamsa a lot of headaches. However, for the Repalli people, Nanda's son has become delightful and enjoying his divine plays. Even though it appears fun to be around Krishna, they are indirectly benefitting due to their direct association with the Lord. It can happen only due to many merits done in their past lives.

Gopika girls who were intensely enjoying the company of Krishna, His temporary absence, even for a few hours, became intolerable. Though not happy with the young Gopika girls playing around Krishna, the town elders had to agree to the ritual that Gopikas performed under Krishna's leadership to reduce and avoid floods and drought. With that pretext, they are coming closer to Krishna and want to fulfill their desires involving Krishna.

The girl's desire to perform the ritual is 'parai', a musical instrument, enough excuse to come and see Krishna. But what they really desire is 'unnai-aruththiththu vandhom,' Krishna only. Hence they say we want you, and you are the only one who can fulfill our desires.

When the Lord is there to protect and take care of the devotees' whole welfare, it appears silly to ask Him to give small, silly material things in life. Does it not show ignorance on the part of the seekers?

Hence the devotees who are knowledgeable seekers do not ask for worldly sense objects but only for the eternal happiness of being associated with Him.

Gopika girls only asked for the musical instrument to satisfy their elders, as they allowed girls to interact with Krishna to perform the ritual. They know that Krishna will fulfill their desires. Hence they '*thiruththakka selvamum saevagamum*', sang and praised His unparallel valor and strength. Immersed in that ecstasy, 'varuththamum theerndhu', forgetting the misery they suffered for not being associated with Him, they praised Him, saying they would enjoy His company now.

Implied meaning:

To reach Bhagavan, in relation to all other means of attaining Him, a direct approach involving complete surrender to Him is the best. In that way, one can attain immediate unification with Him and, in the process, get rid of all the bondages and the associated suffering experience life after life. This simple and direct means that He taught as His final teaching in Geeta helps the Jeeva a secure and permanent above enjoying the eternal, infinite happiness with Him by serving Him to the best one can.

తనుహృద్వాషల సఖ్యమున
	శ్రవణమున దాసత్వమున వందనా
ర్చనముల్ సేవయు నాత్మలో
	నెఱుకయున్ సంకీర్తనల్ చింతనం
బను నీ తొమ్మిది భక్తిమార్గముల
	సర్వాత్మున్ హరిన్నమ్మి స
జ్ఞనుడై యుండుట భద్రమంచు(
	దలతున్ సత్యంబు దైత్యోత్తమా. (Potana)

Thus, the one who follows the path of Bhakti, with complete faith in the Lord, will attain liberation. The Bhaktas know this, and hence they follow.

Many people have described the nature of Mukti in their own way.

కొందరు మిత్తి ముక్తియను
	కొందు రవిద్య తొలంగి పోవుటే
కొందరు ముక్తి యందు ఠిక
	కొందరు జన్మవిముక్తి ముక్త(టే
ర్కొందురు, వారదెట్టు లను
	కొన్నను దివ్యవిభూతియందు గో
వింద యొసంగుమయ్య నిను వే
	డితి నీ పరిచర్య కేశవా. (My Keshavaprapatti)

Thus, in the highest abode (parandhama), being with Paramatma, serving Him, pleasing Him, and enjoying the highest happiness is the very goal for all Jeevas, since we are only part of Him. That is Mukti. To attain that state, of all the paths prescribed in Geeta, the path of complete surrender at the readily available lotus feet of the Lord is the easiest path, for all of us.

Pasuram:

ఒక తల్లి తనయు(డై యొదవి నీవొక రేయి
    యొకతెకు టుడుతడై యొదిగి యొదిగి,
మనికి గిట్టని మామ మదిలోన(బొదలెడి
    తలపుల సెల్లరిత్తల నొనర్చి
కలవరింతయు వంత కలతయు నులుకింత
    యుడివోని కంసుని కడుపులోన
కడివోని టెడిదంపు కారుచిచ్చును(బోలె
    అదిరి నిల్చిన హాటకాంబరుండ
'దేహి' యని వచ్చినారము దేవ దేవ,
    యావు కరుణింప నుతియింతు మేము నీదు
భవ్యసౌభాగ్యసౌశీల్య వైభవముల
    నడగ, సంతాప, మానంద మావహిల్ల.

PASURAM 26

Introduction:

The Gopika girls asking now what they need to performing the ritual.

மாலே! மணிவண்ணா மார்கழி நீராடுவான்
    மேலையார் செய்வனகள் வேண்டுவன கேட்டியேல்
ஞாலத்தையெல்லாம் நடுங்க முரல்வன
    பாலன்ன வண்ணத்துன் பாஞ்சன்னியமே
போல்வன சங்கங்கள் போய்ப்பாடு உடையனவே
    சாலப்பெரும் பறையே பல்லாண்டு இசைப்பாரே
கோல விளக்கே கொடியே விதானமே
    ஆலின் இலையாய் அருள் ஏல் ஓர் எம்பாவாய்

Maalae! Manivannaa! Maargazhi neeraaduvaan

Maelaiyaar seyvanagal vaenduvana kaettiyael

Nyaalaththai ellaam nadunga muralvana

Paal anna vannaththu un paancha sanniyamae

Polvana sankangal poyp paadudaiyanavae

Saalap perum paraiyae pallaandu isaippaarae

Kola vilakkae kodiyae vidhaanamae

Aalin ilaiyaay arulaelor embaavaay (26)

Meaning: Oh! Great Soul! You have great affection for us. Hence you let us see you, got up from sleep and came out, occupied your seat, and were ready to listen to our needs. You let us see by our eyes your beautiful dark blue body. You came and be amidst us. We are very fortunate indeed. For the ritual, we need a conch similar to your Panchajanya conch, musical instruments, singers, those who can sing benedictions (pallandu), and the sacred lights. Please provide us – thus, the Gopica girls requested.

Implied meaning:

The conscious beings, the Jeevas, are part of Paramatma. Caught in the Bhagavan's Maaya, fell from His abode, deluding themselves in the temporary happiness derived by indulging in the sense-pleasures, got into the cycle of karma to janma – or endless birth-death cycle of samsara.

Once they have gained birth as human beings due to merits performed in their past lives, evolving slowly from predominate tamo guna to rajo guna and finally sattvic guna. With the guidance of a proper Acharya or spiritual teacher, they are now trying to acquire the highest state that Jeeva can attain.

'बहूनाम् जन्मनामंते ज्ञानवान् माम् प्रपद्यते'
(Geeta 7:19)).

After many births, Jeeva gets interested in gaining the knowledge to attain moksha. Even to have a such interest is very rare indeed. Even if one desires moksha, they may approach the other small Gods, thinking that these Gods can bless them with moksha. We can find many such kinds of seekers in the world. The other Gods cannot make the seeker cross the ocean of Maaya. Moksha can be gained only by getting over Maaya. That can only be done by surrendering to Lord Narayana.

The killing Shakatasura, drinking the poisonous milk from Putana, killing the Ashvasura, eliminating the wrestlers, Chanura and Mushtika, destroying the ruler of Lanka, Ravana, to protect the sages and saints, taking birth again and again to uplift dharma and destroy adharma, always looking after the welfare of Gods who are committed to Dharma, being born as a young boy, Vamana, and then occupying the entire universe by his three feet, etc., all are done by Shreeman Narayana only. He is the one who takes care of our welfare, giving what we need and taking away what we do not need (yoga and kshema). '*Narayane namkke parai tiruvaan*' – to that supreme Narayana with full faith, Jeeva has to surrender completely to Him to cross this ocean of samsara. Those who surrender entirely to Him, recognizing that it is difficult to cross this incredible maayaa of the Lord by jnana, karma, bhakti, or any other yogas, avoiding all the actions that are against Dharma that take one away from Him, and constantly meditating and worshipping Him and doing actions only that are favorable to Him, and thus approach Him via the Acharya. The Lord will dissolve all his sins and take him into His fold.

He has promised those who have surrendered with utmost devotion that He will take care of their yoga and kshema. 'अहम् त्वाम् सर्वपापेभ्यो मोक्षयिष्यामि मा शुच:' – thus He has promised. Hence, with complete faith in Him, one who surrenders to His holy feet, He will remove all the obstacles in their securing moksha and take them to His abode.

Thus, those who got released from the shackles of this samsara and reached the abode of Paramatma not only enjoy the benefits of being in Vaikunta, they become part of Him and possess the divine ornaments resembling the divine weapons of the Lord. They will also have the divine conch and disc similar to the ones Lord is wearing.

Thus these Jeevas who have reached His abode remain eternally there serving the Lord and not only be with Him but be part of Him, enjoying infinite happiness along with Him.

Pasuram:

తమికా(డ హరిమణిరమణీయ మార్గశి
రస్నాన జపతపాచార పరులు
శిష్టులోనర్చెడిచెయిదమ్ము లర్థమ్ము
లెవ్వినా, ఆలింపు మిందిరేశ
వటపలాశ శయాన నటనావిచక్షణ
స్థిర దద్దరిల్ల శబ్దించునవియు
పాలవన్నెల నీదు పాంచజన్యము(బోలు
కమనీయములు శంఖములు మాకు
నీకు పల్లాండు పాడెడి నెల(తలకును
ననుగుణాంటగు డక్కి, కేతనము కంట
దివ్యయలు మెల్వితానము దివ్యమంగ
శాంగ దయసేయుమా కరుణాంతరంగ.

PASURAM 27

Introduction:

The Gopika girls are requesting from Krishna some auspicious materials needed for the ritual.

கூடாரை வெல்லும் சீர்க் கோவிந்தா உன் தன்னைப்
பாடி பறை கொண்டு யாம் பெறு சம்மானம்
நாடு புகளும் பரிசினால் நன்றாக
சூடகமே தோள் வளையே தோடே செவிப்பூவே
பாடகமே என்றனைய பல்கலனும் யாம் அணிவோம்
ஆடை உடுப்போம் அதன் பின்னே பாற்சோறு
மூட நெய் பெய்து முழங்கை வழிவார
கூடியிருந்து குளிர்ந்து ஏல் ஓர் எம்பாவாய்

Koodaarai vellum seer govindhaa un_dhannaip-
Paadip parai kondu yaam perum sammaanam
Naadu pugazhum parisinaal nanraagach
Choodagamae thol valaiyae thodae sevip poovae
Paadagamae enranaiya palagalanum yaam anivom
Aadai uduppom adhan pinnae paar choru
Mooda ney peydhu muzhangai vazhi vaarak
Koodi irundhu kulirndhaelor embaavaay (27)

Meaning: Oh! Great Soul! The most kind-hearted person! Glorifying you with our prayers using multiple musical instruments and performing the Margasira ritual, we feel that the reception we would receive afterward will be memorable. All the people attending the ritual will also appreciate it. Hence, for the ritual, we need auspicious ornaments that all married ladies could wear, such as bangles for hands, earrings, ornaments that connect earrings and hair buns, bells near the feet, and the appropriate dresses for the ritual.

After the auspicious bath, wearing new clothes, and praying, we want to partake with you in the special food offered at the ritual, which involves rice cooked in milk, with lots of ghee, so much that it will be dripping from the eating hand. That is how we want to enjoy your company.

Implied meaning:

In the last pasuram, how the Jeevas can approach the Lord by surrendering to and associating with Him was described.

For Mukti, or liberation from this samsara, the most beneficial thing that Jeevas gain is the chance to serve the Lord and become happy by making the Lord happy by their service. Jeevas always have to be vigilant to see what makes the Lord happy. The Lord is the Universal male. The rest of the Jeevas are like females. In principle, there are no categories of what gives happiness or sorrow to Him. Even for a realized Jeeva (स्थितप्रज्ञ), it is said that he does not care with something gives happiness or unhappiness or whether something is beneficial or not, etc. सुखदुःखे समे कृत्वा लाभालाभौ जयाजयौ" (Geeta 2:38). His mind does not get perturbed one way or the other. Then what to talk about Paramatma? Does He differentiate what gives happiness, what does not, and what is a gain or loss? He does not care if it is poison or nectar since He pervades everything, as one sees in His Virat swaruupam shown in the 11th Ch. of Geeta.

However, from the point of a devotee, based on his experience, he should determine what is good and what is terrible and do only what is good. It will only help his mind and make it agitation-less. That helps his mind to see the Lord's beauty that permeates everything.

Shabari selected only the sweet and ripe fruits, rejecting those that were not, for offering them to the Lord Shree Ramachandra. The Lord, however, did not care for that but only paid attention to the devotion with which she was serving the fruits. Lakshmana was worried about why she was serving the fruits she had already tasted. Lord only pays attention to the devotion and attitude of service, not what is being served. 'पत्रम् पुष्पम् फलम् तोयम् यो मे भक्त्या प्रयच्छति' (Geeta 9:26). Either fruit, flower, leaf, or even water, whatever is offered with devotion, Lord is ready to take as He pays His attention only to the devotion with which the offer is made. The one who drank poisonous milk of Putana, what is bitter and what is sweet?

Hence, the Gopika girls only desire the auspicious materials based on their experience. They strongly feel that Lord will only appreciate and be happy with the girls wearing bangles, earrings, fresh clothes, etc.

This body is mine. I have to wash it with scented water, decorate it beautifully by applying good-smelling cents and dress beautifully so that others can appreciate my beauty. If that is the attitude, then it only contributes to the ego. And one can get hurt if the others ignore the person or become jealous when one finds another person's body looks more beautiful. Hence such a kind of attitude only increases one's ego. One should eat to live and not live to eat.

One who has surrendered himself fully feels that the body belongs to the Lord. In the Vaishnava tradition, a devotee marks his shoulders with a conch and disk, declaring that the body belongs to the Lord. Therefore any action performed using the body also belongs to the Lord. That forms the essence of Karma yoga too.

In this body, Lord is there as innermost essence. Hence, the body should be treated as a temple. Hence it should be kept clean all the time and decorated beautifully with appropriate ornaments and keeping it trim with proper exercises, etc., so that the Lord inside is happy. Then it is not wrong. Thus, the attitude with which one performs is more important than the action itself. Krishna declares this in Geeta:

अहम् वैश्वानरोभूत्वा प्राणिनाम् देहमाश्रितः।
प्राणापानसमायुक्तः पचाम्यन्नम् चतुर्विधम्॥
(Geeta 15:14)

I, as Vaisvaanara, reside in the bodies of all beings. I am the one who controls all the physiological functions of the body involving prana (breathing), apaana (excretion), samaana (digestion), vyaana (distribution), udaana (upward movement, speech, etc.). Without His help, we cannot even lift our hands or even blink our eyes. Recognition of this fact should make us humble.

Thus wearing decent clothes and ornaments and offering ghee mixed milk rice with full devotion to the Lord and taking part with the Lord is 'sayujyamu', a feeling that one is united with the Lord. Milk rice is symbolic and secondary. 'सोऽश्नुते सर्वान् कामान् सह ब्रह्मणा विपश्चिता' a famous statement by shruti that says that Jeevas enjoy all things along with Paramatma.

Gaining such Mukti or working towards it is the very purpose of taking this birth as a human being. Hence every Jeeva has to work towards this goal.

Pasuram:

కూడని పెరవారి నోడించు టలియు(డా
గోవింద! మేము నిన్ గొలిచి పాడి
కైకొని ధక్క, లోకము లెల్ల (బొగడంగ(
బడయు సన్మానంటు నుడువనిమ్ము
కరకంకణమ్ము లంగదములు కమ్మలు
చెవిపూలు కాలి మంజీరములును
మొదలైన పలునగల్ మురిసి కై సేసికొని
వలిపంపు మేలిదువ్వలువ గట్టి
పాయసాన్నము మునుగంగ నేయివోసి
పిదప నయ్యది మోచేతివెంట గార
మించు రుచిపాకముల నెచ్చరించు కొనుచు
తింద మందరుగూడి యానందమొంద.

PASURAM 28

Introduction:

Gopika girls request Krishna to excuse their mistakes and accept their services.

கறவைகள் பின்சென்று கானம் சேர்ந்து உண்போம்
    அறிவொன்றும் இல்லாத ஆய்க்குலத்து
    உன்தன்னைப்
பிறவி பெருந்தனை புண்ணியம் யாம் உடையோம்
    குறைவொன்றும் இல்லாத கோவிந்தா,
    உன்தன்னோடு
உறவேல் நமக்கு இங்கு ஒழிக்க ஒழியாது
    அறியாத பிள்ளைகளோம் அன்பினால் உன்தன்னைச்
சிறுபேர் அழைத்தனவும் சீறி அருளாதே
    இறைவா! நீ தாராய் பறை ஏல் ஓர் எம்பாவாய்

Karavaigal pin senru kaanam saerndhu unbom

Arivu onrum illaadha aayk kulaththu un_dhannaip

Piravi perundhanaip punniyam yaam udaiyom

Kurai onrum illaadha govindhaa un_dhannodu-

Uravael namakku ingu ozhikka ozhiyaadhu

Ariyaadha pillaigalom anbinaal un_dhannai

Siru paer azhaiththanam seeri arulaadhae

Iraivaa nee thaaraay paraiyaelor embaavaay (28)

Meaning: Oh! Krishna! We are cowherd women. We spend our lives taking calves to forests for them to graze grass and bring them back home. It is our livelihood. We are ignorant of worldly knowledge and are not sophisticated to transact with world affairs. We are blessed that you are born among us.

Nobody can change our relationship with you, soaked with pure innocence and devotion towards you.

Oh! Prince! Being ignorant, not familiar with low and high classifications, only living among Gokula people, behaving ourselves like cows, we do not know your greatness. Hence we called you names! Hai! Krishnaa! Oh! Dear Friend! You Fellow! and in the process, have insulted you. Please do not get angry with us because of these. Please bless us and fulfill our desires.

Implied meaning:

Jeevas are requesting the Paramatma. OH! Lord! We got caught by the Prakruti because of our ignorance. We are behaving like animals without understanding the fundamental truth about you. You are beyond all classifications. To uplift us, you have withdrawn your divine luster by controlling your radiance, leaving your divine abode, and entering the world of this Prakriti, taking the form of a human being.

We are fortunate that You grow up with us from childhood, even though you are the king of the whole universe, creating and dissolving the universes.

एतद्योनीनि भूतानि सर्वाणीत्युपधारय
अहम् कृत्स्नस्य जगतः प्रभवः प्रलयस्तथा|
मत्तः परतरम् नान्यत्किंचिदस्ति धनम्जय.
मयि सर्वमिदम् प्रोतम् सूत्रे मणिगणा इव|
(Geeta 7-7:6)

पिताऽहमहस्य जगतः माताधाता पितामहः
वेद्यम् पवित्रमोंकार ऋक्साम यजुरेवच|

गतिर्भर्ता प्रभु स्साक्षीनिवासः शरणम् सुहृत्
प्रभवः प्रळयः स्थानम् निधानम् बीजमव्ययम्|
(Geeta 18-9:17))

Thus, you have mentioned that you are the creator, sustainer, and dissolver of the entire universe. You are the supreme cause for everything and support the whole universe like the thread in the necklace of pearls. You are the father and mother of the whole universe. The sacred symbol Om-kaara and all the Vedas are you. You are the goal for everyone and the protector and the sustainer for everything. The creation comes from you and gets dissolved into you. Otherwise, how can we know your greatness? We didn't even know who we were until you told us that we are part of you, ममैवांशो जीवलोके जीवभूत स्सनातनः

मनःषष्ठानीद्रियाणि प्रकृतिस्थानि कर्षति||
(Geeta 15:7)

Our relations ships can be expressed in many ways, father-child, protector-protected, sustainer-sustained, husband-wife, knower-known, supporter-supported, soul-body, enjoyer-enjoyed, etc. The interrelation between Paramatma and Jeevatma has been well established. Hence, how can the relationship between the two be broken? Is it breakable at all?

तदहम् त्वद्दते न नाथवान् मद्दते त्वम्
दयनीयवान्नच।
विधिनिर्मित मे तदन्वयम् भगवन्पालय मा स्म
जीहप:॥ (Shree Yamunacharya)

కాన నో జగన్నాథా! నా స్వామీ!
నీకు ననువీడి మరి దయనీయుడొండు
లేడు నీకంటె దయ(జూచువా(డు నాకు
దైవ నిర్ణీతమైన బాంధవ్య మిద్ది
దీని విడనాడ(జూడకో దేవదేవ| (My Yatirajeeyamu)

Please do not try to dismantle the relationship between us. If you leave me, I will become an orphan. If not you, who else is there to protect me? There is no one.

Not only that. Is there anyone else besides me that deserves your protection? If you leave me unprotected, then your kindness will get wasted. Hence, please uplift me from this samsara.

You have earned the name of a very kind-hearted person because you eagerly protected Gajendra and Shabari. It is tough to earn a good name but very easy to lose it. Hence to keep your kind-hearted nature, you have to protect me.

Why should I waste my time in requesting you? We know that you stand by your words at any cost. That full faith I have. You have promised that you will protect all those by wiping out all the sins they have committed if they surrender entirely to you, leaving everything. Therefore I know that you will definitely protect me.

Without recognizing your greatness, thinking that you are also another ordinary human being, due to my ignorance, I have talked some nonsense and insulted you.

सखेति मत्वा प्रसभम् यदुक्तम् हे कृष्ण! हे यादव हे सखेति,
अजानता महिमानम् तवेदम् मया प्रमादात् प्रणयेन वापि.
यच्चापहासार्थं मसत्कृतोऽसि विहारशय्यासन भोजनेषु
एकोऽथवाप्यच्युत तत्समक्षम् तत्क्षामये त्वामहप्रमेयम्|
(Geeta 42-11:41))

Please, I request you to pardon me for my mistakes. OH! Great Soul! Whatever you think is good for me, please bless me with that. I am not qualified to know what is good and bad for me. Due to my bondage to the Prakriti and my delusional indulgence in the sense-pleasures, I cannot judge what is right for me. I am prostrating to you with all my heart. I only feel I want to serve you and do only those who please you. Please accept my surrender and take me to your fold. I am entirely yours.

Pasuram:

ఆలదూడల వెన్క నడవికి(టోవుటే
    దేహ యాత్రోపాధి దేవ మాకు
తెలివిమాలిన గొల్లకులమున దేవర
    పుట్టుట మా పూర్వపుణ్యఫలము
కొఅత యింతయులేని గోవింద మన కున్న
    ఈ బంధమును బాప నెవరితనము?
తెలిసి తెలియక నిన్ను వలపుటలుపునజేసి
    హే కృష్ణ! హే గోప! హే సఖా! య
టంచు బిలిచిన పలుకుల నెంచుకొనక
తెల్లదామర పూవుల(దెగడు కనుల
సంజకెంజాయ సొరనీక సరస లోచ
నాంత కాంతుల(బరపు మా వంతలడగ|

PASURAM 29

Introduction:

Gopika girls say that their visit to Krishna is not just to collect the musical instruments but to express their devotion and prayers to the Lord and surrender themselves to His divine grace.

சிற்றஞ் சிறு காலே வந்துன்னைச் சேவித்து உன்
    பொற்றாமரை அடியே போற்றும் பொருள் கேளாய்!
பெற்றம் மேய்த்து உண்ணும் குலத்தில் பிறந்து நீ
    குற்றேவல் எங்களை கொள்ளாமல் போகாது
இற்றைப் பறை கொள்வான் அன்று காண் கோவிந்தா!
    எற்றைக்கும் ஏழேழ் பிறவிக்கும் உன்தன்னோடு
உற்றோமே யாவோம் உனக்கே நாம் ஆட்செய்வோம்
    மற்றை நம் காமங்கள் மாற்று ஏல் ஓர் எம்பாவாய்

Sitram siru kaalae vandhu unnai saeviththu un-

Potraamarai adiyae potrum porul kaelaay

Petram maeyththu unnum kulaththil pirandhu nee-

Kutraeval engalaik kollaamal pogaadhu

Itraip parai kolvaan anru kaan govindhaa

Etraikkum aezh aezh piravikkum un thannodu-

Utromae aavom unakkae naam aatcheyvom

Matrai nam kaamangal maatraelor embaavaay (29)

Meaning: Oh! Lord! Govinda! We came here in the very early morning, before sunrise, while it was still dark and cold outside, just to be with you.

We have sung divine songs by completely surrounding at your divine golden feet that are very delicate and beautiful like fully bloomed lotus flowers.

We are plain-hearted, simple, innocent Gopa Gopikas. We are honest people living peacefully without any deceptions. We are straightforward people and do not say something and do something else.

We are all mesmerized by your unimaginable beauty, and we only want to serve you in every possible way and be close to you.

Please do not push us away thinking that we are uncivilized cowherd girls and make us go away from here without letting us serve you.

Please do not ask, 'you wanted only conch, disk, umbrella, etc. And just for these, why do you come all the way in the cold, losing your sleep and disregarding that is still dark?' It is just a pretext for us to come and see you. What we really want is not only for this life but want to be near your holy presence, which is beyond the life and death cycle. That we feel is the highest fulfillment of our existence itself.

Just in case we are tempted to go after the sense-objects and otherworldly materials and possessions due to past habits, please bless us that we will be able to cut off those desires in the bud so that our minds are entirely devoted to you.

Implied meaning:

Oh! Paramatma! We do not know what good deeds we have done in the past. Because of those, we are fortunate to have the guidance and blessings of the right teacher, and because of him, we can know and understand your divine nature. Breaking our shackles that have been propelling us to the endless cycle of birth and death and attaining solvation, we have recognized that you, as the supreme God, are the means and goal. Hence we have come with a desperate plea to you, the husband of the auspicious Lakshmi Devi. We surrender ourselves with supreme faith at your holy feet, which are enchanting and holy.

Recognizing that running after the worldly sense objects to obtain temporary pleasures and happiness will only strengthen our bondage to samsara, we left all of them, and recognizing that serving at your holy feet is the very purpose of our existence, and we have come to you.

You are our supreme soul. You have blessed, and are getting constant service from Adisheha, Garuda, Visvaksena, etc., who are eternally liberated souls. We got caught up and bound by Prakriti. We got trapped by our rajas and tamo gunas. However, please do not refuse our services.

You also have taken a human birth out of your will as part of your leela. The external outer coverings are not important to you. Yet, you took different external forms – Matsya (fish), Kurma (tortoise), Varaha (pig), Narasimha (half lion and half human), etc., to solve the problems.

Hence ignoring our external forms, recognizing our devotion and our desperate plea, please bless us by accepting our services.

सत्यम् शपेवारण शैलनाथ वैकुंठवासेऽपि
नमेऽभिलाषः - (Vedanta Deshika)

Thus it is a blessing to serve you, and that is only our desire, and we have no desire even to attain some supreme abode. We can remain on this earth or take as many lives as possible, *etraikkum aezh aezh piravikkum un thannodu utromae aavom unakkae naam aatcheyvom*', as long as we are blessed to serve you all the time.

'एतद्देहावसाने माम् त्वत्पादम् प्रापय स्वयम्' – Even our request for moksha is only to serve your holy feet. That we feel is essential for all Jeevas. This service can be done there in the highest abode or here itself remaining on this earth. It is the same. Hence Kulashekhara Alwar prays that all he wants is that he be blessed to have devotion towards him life after life.

भावे भावे हृदयभवने भावयेयम् भवंतम्
एतत्प्रार्थ्यम् मम बहु मतम् जन्म जन्मांतरेऽपि
त्वत् पादांभोरुहयुगगता निश्चला भक्ति रस्तु.
(Mukundamala)

That bhakti is also in the form of desire only to serve the Lord. However many lives it is going to be, all we desire is only to serve you all the time. *matrai nam kaamangal maatraelor*' Please make sure we do not get any other desires. – Thus, the Gopika girls are praying to Lord Krishna.

Pasuram:

సెచ్చెలిపిండుతో వచ్చి వేగకమున్న
    నిన్ను సంసేవించి నీ తిరువడి
పొందామరలదోయి(టొగడుటలో గల
    భావంటు నాలింపు దేవదేవ,
పశులమేపి భుజించు వంశాన జనియించి
    వారింపరాదు గోపాల, మాదు
కైంకర్యములను, డక్కంగొంటకై కాదు
    సుమ్ము మా యీ రాక శోభనాంగ!
పూని యేడేడుజన్మాలకేని నీదు
పాదపంకేజ దాస్యతత్వరల మన్య
చింతలేవియు మామది(జేర నీకు
పరమ పావన భవదీయపాద మాన|

PASURAM 30

Introduction:

Discusses the benefits of the Pasuram recital and performing the Margasira ritual during the Margasira month.

வங்கக் கடல் கடைந்த மாதவனைக் கேசவனை
    திங்கள் திருமுகத்துச் சேயிழையார் சென்று
    இறைஞ்சி
அங்கு அப்பறை கொண்ட ஆற்றை அணிபுதுவைப்
    பைங்கமலத் தண்தெரியல் பட்டர் பிரான் கோதை
    சொன்ன
சங்கத் தமிழ் மாலை முப்பதும் தப்பாமே
    இங்கு இப்பரிசு உறைப்பார் ஈரிரண்டு மால் வரைத்
    தோள்
செங்கன் திருமுகத்துச் செல்வத் திருமாலால்
    எங்கும் திருவருள் பெற்று இன்புறுவர் எம்பாவாய்

Vangak kadal kadaindha maadhavanai kaesavanai
Thingal thirumugaththu saey izhaiyaar senru irainchi
Angap parai konda aatrai ani pudhuvaip-
Painkamalath than theriyal battar piraan kodhai sonna
Sangath thamizh maalai muppadhum thappaamae
Ingu ipparisuraippaar eerirandu maal varaiththol
Sengan thirumugaththuch chelvath thirumaalaal
Engum thiruvarul petru inburuvar embaavaay (30)

Meaning: Bhagavan is the cause for the creation, sustenance, and dissolution of the Universe. Because of Him, only these entire inert and conscious beings are created. If one asks who created Bhagavan? It is said that He, being beginningless, cannot be created nor can be dissolved. If we say, He was also a product of creation; then the question arises who created Him and if there is another Bhagavan, who created that Bhagavan? Thus, it leads to an infinite regress. Hence, we must accept that Bhagavan is beginningless and, therefore, endless. Hence we call Bhagavan a causeless cause.

The question then is – who is the Bhagavan? Is He Lord Shiva, Brahmaji, or Shree Vishnu? Or is it some kind of power? Is it Nature or Prakriti, as the famous Scientist Steven Hopkin once declared? This question keeps coming. Who is going to answer this question? Can a human being find out with his limited intellect? What is the answer to this question?

For the answer, we have to go to Shastras, which can tell us that these things can not be established by objective analysis that all the objective sciences are involved. Objective sciences can only analyze objectifiable entities using objective tools. They cannot analyze the consciousness which all living beings have. They cannot even analyze the mind or a thought, which they use to analyze everything else. There are a lot of theories about the mind, by philosophers on one side and psychologists on the other. There are also many speculative theories that one can find in the 'Cognitive Sciences' Journals. They cannot even analyze what Life is.

Hence to find out the answers, we have to turn to Shastras, which are Vedas that are considered beginningless or apousheyam or not authored by a human being. They talk about life before birth and, therefore, life after birth and creator and creation. These are revelations to the meditative minds of the Sages (scientists of the yore), which they passed it on to their disciples, who intern passed it on to their disciples by word of mouth. Since they heard, the Vedas are called shrutis.

Veda means knowledge derived from the root, vid, meaning to know. Science also means knowledge derived from the root, *scire*, meaning to know. In contrast to objective sciences, Vedas analyze the subject, the inquirer or Jeeva, and his relationship with Nature or Prakruti, which is inert. 'वेदैः पश्यंति पंडिताः' The wise people learn what is to be known from Vedas, which cannot be known otherwise.

However, some do not consider Vedas are the means of knowledge of the absolute. Many think that their religion is most important and what their teachers teach is only correct. Any teacher is a human being who cannot be the source of knowledge that is beyond human comprehension. Instead of pramaa, a true knowledge, it can be a bhramaa or knowledge which can be falsified. We cannot do much about their beliefs.

आहुर्वेदा समाजम् कतिचन, कतिचाराजकम्
विश्वमेतत्
राजन्वत्केचि दीशम् गुणिनमपि गुणैस्तम्
दरिद्राणमाहुः
भिक्षावन्ये सुराजम् भवमिति च जडास्ते
तिलातल्यकार्षुः
ये ते श्रीरंग हम्र्यांगण कनकलतेन क्षणम्
लक्ष्यमासन्। (Shree Gunaratnaprakasham-
Parasar Bhattar)

Some say that universe came by itself. There is no other person who created or who is the master of this. Others say there is a creator and master of this Universe. He is there, but He is without any attributes and a non-doer. Some argue that the creator is a bikshaka or asks for alms (Lord Shiva). Lord Shiva is the supreme Lord. Oh! Goddess Lakshmi, without your blessings, all these people argue and fight.

'वेदान्ता स्तत्त्वचिन्ताम् मुरभिदुरसि यत्पादचिह्ने तरंति'-Who is Paramatma if one wants to inquire, then He is the one who has Lakshmi 's symbol carrying on His chest. Hence the Purushottama is defined in the purushasuktam as 'ह्रीश्चते लक्षीश्च पत्न्यौ' -He is the husband of Lakshmi Devi. That provides the required pramaana or means of knowledge to who is Paramatma. That Madhava (husband of maa = Lakshmi) is Keshava. Hence Lord Shiva says to Lord Vishnu

क इति ब्रह्मणो नाम ईशोहम् सर्वदेहिनाम्,
आवाम् तवांगे संभूतौ तस्मात् केशवनामभाक्|

Thus, he explained the etymology of Keshava. कः is Brahmaji's name. I am Iswara – we both are born from you. Since you are the cause for both of us, you are called Keshava. Also, Keshava means the person with beautiful hair and one who killed the Rakshasa by the name 'Keshi'.

The creation and dissolution portfolios were handed over to Brahmaji and Shivaji. Since they are in charge of creation and dissolution, and responsible for both of them is the husband of Lakshmi – thus, both Brahmanji and Shivaji themselves are praising Lord Vishnu; what to talk about the Gopika girls? What is to be surprised if they praise Lord Krishna in that way?

Those Gopika girls are very calm and serene, with beautiful faces resembling the full moon. That serene beauty itself is their unparalleled ornament. Such girls went to Govinda and praised Him as *'maadhavanai kaesavanai'* .

Why should we praise the Lord? – a rational intellect can ask. It is not that He wants to be praised. It is like calling a multi-billionaire –Oh! Great millionaire! In essence, the one who is infinite, anything we say will be less than what He is. Thus praising is not for His sake but for our sake. In that way, we recognize the infinite glory of the Lord using our limited intellect – which makes us humble with our ego surrendered. It is said that even

Brahma and Iswara praised the glory of the Lord as the protector. Hence approaching the Lord for protection is our recognition that He is the real protector.

Who is He to protect us? If someone asks, Gopika girls say, *'vangak kadal kadaindha maadhavanai'*, He is the one who put uncontrollable waves of the Ocean under control. In the war between Gods and the demons, on both sides,, many were getting killed. However, the teaches of demons, Sukracharya, was using 'Mrutasanjeevani' to make the dead demons alive again who can fight. There was no one to save the Gods. Hence to protect them, Lard Narayana asked them to churn the ocean to get Amrutam, or divine nectar, which makes them death-free. For this Lord has to control the enormous waves of the Ocean.

If Gods and demons were churning the Ocean, what did Narayana do? He took the form of a tortoise and supported the mountain they were using to churn the Ocean. Without His help, they could not have done it. When the nectar was produced, the demons tried to steal it from the Gods. Lord took the form of an enchanting Mohini, lured demons, took the nectar away, and distributed it to Gods. Thus, the Lord is constantly protecting the devotees, sometimes even taking odd forms to get the work done that helps to establish Dharma or order in the universe.

That Lord, the husband of Goddess Lakshmi, is now born as Lord Krishna. How the Gopika girls praise Him and how they achieved not only the things they needed to live in this world but also the permanent abode in the life after; Goda Devi has described all these in these 30 Pasurams. She wrote in Tamil that local people could easily understand and chant, thus blessing them for generations to come.

Goda Devi is the daughter of the well-known Perialwar, Vishnuchitta, from Shree Villiputtur. He used to worship the Lord by decorating him with a beautiful garland made every day with freshly bloomed flowers from his garden. He, by God's grace, established in the Royal place Shree Vishnu's symbolic emblem, thus providing the moral strength for the number of various victories of that Kin. He also composed 'Pallandu Pallandu' salutations for the Lord that are now being chanted in every Vaishnava Temple. He offered his daughter, Goda Devi, in marriage to Shree Ranganatha and thus became a father-in-law of the Lord.

Vishnuchitta found his daughter, Goda Devi, as a baby in his Tulasi Gardon. She is considered as the incarnation of Goddes Earth or Bhudevi. She loved only the Lord and became His lover. She used to decorate herself first with the Garland that Vishuchitta was offering to the Lord, without his knowledge, before he took it to the temple for the Lord. Lord loved the Garland more since it was worn before by Goda Devi.

That Goddess Goda Devi is the composer of this Tiruppavai, consisting of 30 pasurams, written in the language and style that even the local people could understand and sing with devotion, particularly during the 30 days of Margasira month (the middle of December to the middle of January). Whoever chants this Tiruppavai daily will receive the following.

He will get the blessings of Lord Narayana, who is ever brilliant, the one with beautiful fully bloomed lotus eyes, with the face that exhibits the one who is the master of all arts and that is more pleasingly brilliant than the full moon, one who is carrying the brilliant Panchajanya Conch, Sudarshana Disk, Koumodaki Gada (mace), Nandaka sward, etc. to protect the devotees as well as to bless them.

श्रीमद्भागवतार्चनम् भगवत पूजाविधेरुत्तमम्
श्रीविष्णोरवमाननाद्गुरुतरम् श्रीवैष्णवोल्लंघनम्
तीर्थादच्युतपादजाद्गुरुतरम् तीर्थम् तदीयांघ्रिजम्
तस्मान्नित्यमतंद्रितो भव सदा तेषाम् समाराधने।

The Lord appreciates the devotees who serve His other devotees that have surrendered to Him rather than serving Him directly. He also gets angrier with those who abuse His devotees than those who directly abuse Him. His love for his devotees is even more than any mother's love for her children. Hence the Lord appreciates those who revere Goda Devi and her compositions and chant daily with devotion more than those who pray to Him directly.

Hence, OH! Devotees of the Lord! Please know that without the grace of the Lord, we cannot cross this ocean of samsara. Hence to earn His grace, we have to serve His devotees, the devotees of His devotees, ignoring in the process any of their worldly faults, without insulting them and only considering their high qualities, following their footsteps in their devotion to the Lord. Hence Acharyas have taught the above as

यान्यनवद्यानि कर्मणि। तानि सेवित व्यानि। नो इतराणि। यान्यस्माकगं सुचरितानि। तानित्वयोपास्यानि नो इतराणि। (Taittiriya Upanishat)

Thus, following the methods prescribed by our Acharyas, let us all serve and be blessed with the grace of Sreeman Narayana.

Pasuram:

లొలొర్మి మాలికాజాల పారావార
మదనుని కేశవు మామహిహకు
రాకానిశాకాంత రమణీయ ముఖు లలం
కారాంచితలు గొల్ల కన్నె లచట
పాడి వాంఛితములఁ టడసిన వార్త ను
పెరియాళువారుల ప్రియతనూజ
శ్రీవిల్లి పుత్తూరు చెడెలలో మిన్న
గోద తమిళమునఁ గూర్చినట్టి
తెనుగుననను శేషదాసుఁడు తీర్చినట్టి
పద్ధియంటుల నిచ్చ ముప్పదియు విడక
చదువువానిని గరుణించు శౌరి చంద్ర
వదను(డట్టాక్షు(డాజానుబాహు వెపుడు.

EPILOGUE

This completes the extensive commentary in Telugu by the grandson of Shree Kuntimaddi Sreenivasacharya, son of Seshamma and Rangacharya, adopted son of Venkatarangacharya, servant of the lotus feet of Shree Hayavadana Shree Madabhinava Ranganatha Swami, Sesha Dasa (Kuntimaddi Seshasarma), on Shree Goda Divi's Tiruppavai.

The English translation of the original book entitled Melinomu, published by Tirumala Tirupati Devasthanam (TTD), is done by the son of the author, Kuntimaddi Sadananda, with the help of his siblings, Smt. Sowdamini and Sudhasindhu.

- सर्वम् श्रीकृष्णार्पणमस्तु

www.ingramcontent.com/pod-product-compliance
Lightning Source LLC
Chambersburg PA
CBHW051220130726
47988CB00001B/151